CHECKPOINT

CHECKPOINT

ROD HURON

Tyndale House
Publishers, Inc.
Wheaton, Illinois

Library of Congress
Catalog Card Number 78-65905
ISBN 0-8423-0231-X
Copyright © 1979
by Rod Huron
First printing,
April 1979.
Printed in the
United States of America.

CHECKPOINT

Friday afternoon, December 21

PEACE BRIDGE
50 KILOMETRES

"Fifty k's to the Peace Bridge," Gregg read as the highway sign flashed by. "Thirty minutes to the great Democratic Republic of America."

Heather, Gregg's soft and lovely wife as of four months ago, squirmed in her seat, trying to be comfortable.

Momentarily taking his eyes off the road, Gregg looked over at her. "Nervous?"

She slumped into the seat and looked back at him, answering with silence. Then, "Will they search us, love?"

Gregg shrugged. "Maybe. We won't really know until we get there. Don't worry though; we'll be all right."

Their white Volvo wagon gained slowly on a big tanker. Traffic in both directions was sparse. Was this the calm before the storm? Gregg wondered.

Clouds in the west threatened to engulf the fading winter day. The few drivers still on the road seemed to be hurrying for shelter from the wind and coming darkness. Except for occasional patches of pure snow, the earth and sky merged into a drab palette of grays and browns.

Checking his rear view mirror, Gregg fingertipped the turn signal and pulled out into the passing lane. "Okay, buddy," he said, "here I come. The Queen E's part mine, too."

Though their windows were closed, the truck's noise easily smothered conversation and momentarily drowned out the turn signal's tick-tick. Heather relaxed when Gregg eased back into the right hand lane.

"Sure hard to keep it down to 100 k's," he complained, "but we don't want to get picked up now. Not here."

"Better here than down there," she corrected him.

"Better not at all."

At Niagara Falls the Skylon poked its well-lit head over the horizon, a cheerful contrast to the pallid sky. Gregg took the Fort Erie ramp, bypassing the Falls.

"There's Honeymoon City, Heather. If we'd come down here instead of renting the cottage, you would have already seen the border."

Her answer was emphatic. "I didn't want to."

"Neither did I, hon." He touched her hand. "Barbed wire and searchlights aren't my idea of a honeymoon, either."

Heather shuddered.

"You know," he went on, "I'd rather you be with me than with some ugly border guard anyway."

She grimaced. "Oh, love, don't talk like that. Not even in jesting." Her voice revealed her fear.

"Sorry. I'll bet the honeymoon business isn't all that good since the changeover anyway." He turned on the headlights to fight the coming darkness.

"Do you think we'll have snow?"

"I hope so. Or maybe some sleet."

"Is it better to come to the border when the weather's bad?"

Gregg hesitated before answering. "I guess so. They're not usually as careful. I know they don't like to be out in the rain. I don't think they would like snow, either."

Heather thought for a while, then asked, "Have you crossed at this time of year before?"

He shook his head. "I've always gone over during the summer. It's easier when there are more people crossing, more travelers. There's usually a big lineup and they don't inspect as carefully. They don't have time to."

Glancing at his watch, he told her, "Turn on the radio and see what weather is expected."

A blast of rock music answered Heather's touch. "Get that off. I'm not in the mood for that now."

Heather kept pushing buttons until she found CFRB, which offered a recital of the day's trouble in the Middle East, a word from Parliament Hill, news of a bank robbery, and several lesser items. Then: "Weather for Metro Toronto and vicinity will be snow squalls tonight, with winds northerly from fifteen to twenty-five and a low overnight of minus seven. Present temperature minus two; minus four at the airport."

Heather reached down to turn off the radio, but Gregg stopped her. "Leave it on. It looks more natural."

Within minutes the first white flecks minced across their headlight beams. Soon it was snowing hard, forcing Gregg to slow down because of the limited visibility. For several kilometers neither he nor Heather spoke, carried along with the sounds of spray and the wipers' soft staccato. The radio whispered in the background.

Gregg asked, "Want to stop before we cross? It might take an hour. Maybe longer."

"No, I'm all right. Let's go ahead."

Reaching over he took her hand in his. She seemed so fragile. "Sure glad you're along this time," he said, troubled by the slight catch in his voice.

She turned to face him. "Me, too. That is, I think I am. I wouldn't want you to come by yourself. Not now."

"Worrier." He tried to laugh, but couldn't. "It'll be all right. You'll see."

"That's it, isn't it?" she asked suddenly, staring out the windshield.

"That's it."

Heather leaned forward and tried to pierce the blowing lace moving across her line of vision. Pressing her forehead against the glass, she cupped her hands around her eyes to block out reflections. Vaguely she could make out the shape of several buildings.

Just then their headlights picked up a huge sign. Heather shivered as she read the warning reflected back at her:

NOTICE
PERSONS WITHOUT PROPER DOCUMENTS
MAY NOT PROCEED
BEYOND THIS POINT

"Don't worry," Gregg tried to reassure her. "I've got all the papers. We're all set."

"Whatever you say, love," she said, so low he could hardly hear her.

Now Heather could identify the long row of customs booths stretching across the broad plaza. The snow was painting everything white and clean under the floodlights. Most of the booths were closed; hardly anyone was around. Lights in a low building to the right showed four or five people working inside. The CUSTOMS—DOUANES sign was almost covered.

The Volvo splashed up to a booth. Gregg rolled down his window and quickly drew back from the pelting snow and wind.

Stooping to look inside the car, the customs officer noticed Heather and touched gloved fingers to his cap.

"Leaving us, eh?" he asked as Gregg handed over their passports and other papers.

"Hope not. Going down for Christmas."

The officer studied the papers for a moment, then looked up at Gregg.

"Looks as if you came over before the big change."

"Yes, sir," Gregg answered. Glancing at Heather, he added, "Glad I did, too, for lots of reasons."

"Yes," the officer agreed, "I can see that."

He stepped back inside the booth, stamped each form, and brought the papers back to the car.

"I'll ask you for your own safety: Are you carrying any liquor? cigarettes? firearms? ammunition?"

Gregg shook his head each time. The officer stepped back, touched his cap again, and motioned them on.

"No ammunition, Gregg?" Heather ventured as they pulled away.

"Not the kind he meant," said Gregg and managed a

weak smile. They were just starting up the bridge ramp when Heather first saw the guards at the halfway point, their post illuminated by powerful floodlights.

"Gregg, I'm scared."

"You pray," he told her, "and I'll do the talking." Pointing to the side, he continued, "You might not be able to see them in this snow, but they have patrol boats on the river. They can't come much farther than this, because the current from the Falls is too swift even for their supercharged boats. A lot of people have tried to cross along here, but most of them have gone over the Falls. Once in a while somebody makes it. A few years ago choppers were used to fly tourists over the Falls. Now they look for escapees."

Heather took a deep breath as they slowly approached the international boundary checkpoint and the first armed guards. She looked back longingly at the Canadian flag flying beside the U.N. and D.R.A. banners. She shivered at the sight of the heavy fencing closing them in, with four rows of barbed wire along the top.

The approach plaza was lit as bright as daylight, in spite of the blowing waves of snow. Several transports waited in a truck lane. Three cars were lined up ahead of theirs as Gregg slowed and stopped. To their left two guards patrolled side by side.

"Gregg." Heather pointed and instantly lowered her voice, as if the guards could hear. "Is that . . . is that a gun?"

"They both have guns," Gregg answered. "The guy with the dog has his over his shoulder. They're automatics. Pull the trigger and they'll empty a clip like a machine gun." After a long pause, Gregg said, "I can't see it in this snow, but over there a ways is a church they closed down and turned into an army barracks."

"It's awful." Heather felt so much, could say so little.

Shadowy figures moved near the fence. Heather noticed several gaunt steel towers with a small building perched high on top of each one.

"Are those watchtowers?"

"Two men in each one," Gregg answered, "watching everything that moves down here to make sure nothing gets away from them."

"It's like another world, isn't it, Gregg?"

"I've seen this place with cars backed up halfway across the bridge. That was before the change. Now look at it. There's nobody here."

The first two cars had been inspected while they waited and had moved on. Now the car ahead of them, a Chevy bearing a New York license, inched into place. A guard in a dark green uniform motioned for Gregg to pull in close behind. Gregg did so, then reached down to turn off the motor.

"Don't, love. I feel so cold. Leave the wipers on, too. I want to see what is going on."

"You see the guard in the booth?"

Heather nodded.

"He's asking them questions and checking their passports against a computer. He's probably already checked their license plate. If they're on the unwelcome file, it'll show up and he won't let them across. Of course, these guys are Americans from New York, but they could be in trouble if he's got something on file against them. He can refuse anyone permission to cross, and all they can do is turn around and go back."

"So the ones in the green uniforms are the ones we have to watch?"

"No," Gregg replied, gesturing slightly to two figures standing in the shadows, out of the wind. "The ones we have to watch are those two in the black overcoats. They do the inspecting."

As if on cue the raven-coated figures stepped away from the guard building and approached the Chevy. They made the driver get out and open the trunk, then stand to one side while they poked among the suitcases and spare tire.

Both Black Overcoats seemed oblivious to the snow. The driver shifted from one foot to the other, his heavy jacket hunched up around his ears. Pointing, one of the inspectors directed him to take out a large suitcase and open it on the low platform next to the booth.

The officer methodically checked through the suitcase piece by piece. Underclothes, shirts, socks, hair dressing—the hands missed nothing, fingering and searching.

The second official stood back and stared at the driver, searching for any sign that might betray him.

Watching them, Gregg muttered, "That man's stuff is getting wet, but those guys couldn't care less. Just because they're afraid he'll bring something back."

"Gregg," Heather pleaded, "don't. What if they hear you?"

Control, stay in control, Gregg told himself. *Don't ruin this mission before it gets started.*

The guards moved over to the car to begin their search there. The driver brushed the snow off his clothes and returned the suitcase to the trunk. Snow showered onto his legs and shoes when he slammed the lid.

Both Black Overcoats were now probing around the back seat and feeling underneath the front seat and along the floor.

One of them told the driver to ask his wife and daughter to get out of the car. They huddled against the side of the booth for protection.

"Gregg, what is that guard doing?"

One of the men had taken a shiny object from his coat and was tapping the metal underneath the Chevy!

"He's looking for secret compartments," Gregg said slowly, wishing Heather hadn't noticed. "If it doesn't sound right, they'll take the car away and drill holes to see if the guy's carrying anything he's not supposed to."

"What if . . ."

"Relax. The Lord will take care of us. You'll see." Gregg wished he felt as confident as he sounded.

Heather's eyes were riveted to the unfolding drama up ahead. The car was warm with its heater running, motor idling, wipers swishing the melting flakes from their windshield to provide a peephole in their protective steel cocoon. At least protective for now.

The family ahead of them had no such sanctuary. Heather watched the father go around to his wife and daughter, wrapping his coat around the little girl, trying to keep her warm. Heather could see her frail body shaking. She knew the child was shivering from more than cold.

The two vultures finished their inspection by making the driver open the hood so they could look inside the engine compartment. Satisfied, they motioned the family back into their car and toward the exit to the highway.

"We're next," said Gregg, pulling up to the guard in a green uniform. Gregg rolled down his window and shut off the motor. Heather reached for her coat from the back seat, to ward off the cold and her fear.

"Papers." The official's demanding tone was ominous.

Gregg handed over their passports and visas.

"One Canadian, one American. You a citizen of the D.R.A.?" He looked at Gregg.

Gregg chose his words carefully. "Sir, it wasn't the Democratic Republic of America when I came to Canada."

The guard wasn't satisfied.

"That's not what I asked you."

Gregg kept his tone respectful. "You have my passport, sir. It answers your question."

Ignoring Gregg's response, the official continued his cold questioning. "Purpose of visit?"

"We're going to see my family. I want them to meet Heather."

"What proof do you have of your marriage?"

"Her passport, sir."

"Nothing else? No certificate?"

Gregg glanced hopefully over at Heather, but she shook her head.

"No, sir. That's all we have."

Stern D.R.A. eyes glared at the young couple, then turned to their documents. Thumbing through them, the guard turned to the console beside him and tapped several keys. For a few moments he stared into the screen, then, satisfied, handed the papers back to Gregg and nodded to the guards in the black coats.

Anticipating the officers' order, Gregg got out of the car.

"The tailgate, please." The toneless voice was commanding, insistent.

Snow spattered on Gregg's plastic suitcover as the rear

door came up. Black Coat leaned over, ran his hand over the plastic, pressed down several times, then inserted his hand between the larger suitcase and the overnighter.

"Is there a compartment here?"

"Yes," Gregg answered and started taking things out and setting them on the platform. With the suitcase and overnighter and the plastic suitcarrier out of the way, Gregg uncovered a small cargo area under the floor. Glancing at the shoes, Black Coat turned to the packages and wanted to know what they were.

"Presents," Gregg began, "for my family. I'll be glad to show you what's in them."

As he reached for a red-wrapped box, he frantically told himself, *My hand is not shaking, my hand is not shaking.* The inspector was not interested in the package, however, and instructed Gregg to shut the lid. Then he pointed to a cardboard box nestled against the back of the rear seat.

"What's in there?" Still the expressionless, insistent demand.

Gregg wrestled the box out to where the guard could look inside. "It's motor oil. I change my own oil and keep some in the car. Those pieces of carpet are in case we get stuck in the snow, to put under the back wheels."

Black Coat turned to the items on the platform. His partner stood silently by, intent on Gregg's every gesture, every move.

"What's in the suitcase?"

"Personal things."

"That's all?"

"Yes, sir."

"I want to see."

Several minutes later Gregg lifted the suitcase back into the wagon.

Now Black Coat opened the rear door on Heather's side and ran his hand beneath the front seats and across the seat backs. He asked Heather to step out, inspected the glove compartment, pressed down several times on her seat cushion, then motioned for her to get back in.

"That's all. You're through."

Taking his time, Gregg took back his papers, laid his coat

across the back seat, got into the car, and started the engine.

"That heater sure feels good," he said, rubbing his hands together and reaching for the transmission selector.

They were on the skyway before Heather asked, "Where were they, Gregg?"

He feigned innocence, then grinned, then laughed.

"I told you we'd see a miracle!" His unrestrained enthusiasm made him speak a little too loudly, but Heather didn't mind. "Where was the only place the guard didn't look? There are 800 Bibles under the back seat and he never found them. And 200 more in the spare tire well. Now all we've got to do is get them where they're supposed to go." *All,* Gregg thought. *Just give them away without getting caught.*

"When do we deliver them?"

He responded, perhaps too quickly, "As soon as we can, just as soon as we can. Maybe some of them tomorrow."

Two hours later in Washington, D.C., a Security Department executive, a sweating mound of flesh surrounded by clouds of cigar smoke, pored over the latest printouts from points of entry around the country. Squinting through clouds of smoke, he surveyed the information sheets line by line.

One name stopped him in his tracks. His beefy right hand grabbed the desk phone, his thick lips spat orders to the girl in the outer office.

"Get me Larry in Columbus, Ohio. I want to talk to him personally."

"Sir . . ."

"I know what time it is, get him on the phone. I'll hold."

Still clutching the phone, he shifted his chair around and punched several buttons on the console beside his desk. He stared at the screen while the picture formed. Reading the flickering green words and numbers, he scowled and sucked furiously on his cigar. His call went through almost immediately.

"Larry? This is Bert Wilson."

Wilson gave his subordinate a moment to realize the significance of Washington's calling him personally rather than relaying through the usual channels. He tore off the data sheet and held it as he talked.

"I have a suspect car I want you to put a unit on when they come through. I would guess they're on I-90. The printout shows he comes that way every time.

"It's a white Volvo wagon, Ontario license 284-BRX. Believed occupied by a male and female, Gregg and Heather Richards. The sheet says he was born in Ohio, moved to Canada as landed immigrant when his father was transferred to Toronto. Since then he's been back a total of six times.

"He visited New York, Pennsylvania, Ohio, once to Kentucky and Tennessee, one trip across to Denver and back. Listed as a teacher. Border report says they've been married just a few weeks. I want you to find out where he goes, who he sees. I want to know why he keeps coming back over here. Keep your man out of sight, and let me know what you find out."

Saturday morning, December 22

"Don't look around," Gregg muttered softly, lifting a forkful of scrambled eggs to his mouth, "but we've got an audience. The manager is drilling holes through us. Through you, at least."

The smooth motion of Heather's wrist froze for an instant before she continued to spread the jelly on the piece of toast held delicately in her left hand. Finished, she deliberately tore off a little bite and reached for her cup.

"Are you positive, love?"

Heather's voice was pleasant, casual. Any of the three or four other customers hearing her and watching her face would have thought she and Gregg were exchanging wife-husband banalities.

Gregg finished his coffee and turned around, raising his voice slightly. "Wonder if I could get more coffee? I don't know where the waitress went to."

Heather took the cue and looked around the dingy room. Walls once cream colored were several shades darker now. Peeling plaster and streaks along the back wall indicated a leak overhead. Accumulated grime smudged the chrome pass-through to the kitchen. The grill man, visible through the opening, matched the decor. Seeing his uncombed hair and wrinkled smock made Heather more aware of the stale odor of cooking grease.

From his post behind the cash register the manager still watched.

Their waitress reappeared, bearing a steaming pitcher. "More coffee?"

"Yes, please," answered Gregg. Sliding Heather's cup and saucer over, he asked, "Could we have some more tea, also?"

"I'll bring you more hot water," the girl answered, taking the little metal teapot with her.

After the waitress had gone, Gregg leaned closer to his wife. "You Canadians," he teased quietly, "you and your tea."

Her eyes teased back. "It's better than coffee."

"You ought to try this stuff. It'll make a believer out of you."

She leaned her face closer to his and whispered, "I am already a believer, dear."

"So you are," Gregg answered slowly. "So am I, which is why we're here."

He sat looking at Heather while she finished her breakfast. Watching her dainty fingers handle her knife and fork, he suddenly realized what had drawn the manager's attention. Gingerly Heather impaled a morsel of ham with her fork, and with the sure motion of her right wrist cut the piece in two. After she had finished the cut, instead of laying her knife down she used it to urge the morsel onto her fork and into her mouth.

She looked up to find Gregg staring at her. "What's the matter?"

Gregg's eyes pointed to her hands poised above her plate, knife still lightly held in her right hand, fork in her left, tines upside down.

"Don't change now," Gregg told her, almost in a whisper. "He's still keeping his eye on us."

Moments later, walking through the lobby, Gregg whispered in his wife's ear, "I don't know whether that guy was giving you the eye or whether he was suspicious, but you've got to start eating like an American."

"I'll try."

In their room Gregg walked over to their open suitcase on the wall table. He stared intently for a few seconds, then explained in a low voice, "I arranged things so I'd know if we had visitors. See this?" He tapped the case for his electric razor. "I lined this up so it touched here"—he pointed to the sleeve of his pajamas—"and here"—the metal trim around the suitcase lid.

"They tried to put everything back like it was." Emptying the contents of the suitcase onto the bed, he took a quick inventory. "The alarm clock is gone."

Looking through her things, she added, "I'm missing two packages of pantyhose and my perfume." Suddenly uneasy, she asked, "What should we do?"

"We're not going to do anything. It may have just been the maid. Either way we're not going to the police."

"You didn't have anything . . .?"

"No, there wasn't anything in there anyway." Looking up at the ceiling, he repeated, louder this time, "We didn't have anything in it."

"Gregg." Near panic, she moved to put her hand over his mouth.

He put his arms around her and whispered, "Sorry, hon. I'll be careful. I promise."

Outside, last night's snow had laid four inches of softness across everything. Gregg could see that their car was undisturbed. Not a footprint marred the smooth contours windblown around the vehicle.

The highway crews had already cleared the main roads, so they had no trouble getting on their way. The dashboard clock showed 1047 when they reached the Pennsylvania border.

"They have guards here, too?" Heather asked in surprise as Gregg pulled into place at the end of the line.

"They have a checkpoint at every state line," he answered. "Those aren't state troopers, either. Those guys are federal officers, specially trained by the U.S. government, or I should say D.R.A. government."

"Barbed wire here too, eh?"

"The border used to be a red line on a map. Not any more."

"Are they all like this?"

"All the ones I've been to."

They worked their way forward as cars in front of them were cleared.

"This is their way of checking on who's going where. When we go through they'll enter our number into the central computer in Washington."

Heather was shocked. "They do this to Americans, too?"

"To everybody. You can't pick up and move like people used to. If you're in New York, you stay in New York unless you get permission."

As Gregg eased the Volvo up to the checkpoint, Heather saw an officer look at their license plate, then go to work on a control panel beside him.

"Welcome to Pennsylvania," said the guard as he stepped out of his cubicle and stooped to look inside the car. Gregg handed him their passports and visas.

"How long will you be in Pennsylvania?"

"Just today, sir. Could we have a transit pass?"

The officer stepped inside his booth, selected a stamp from several hanging along the wall, stamped both sets of papers, scribbled his initials across each visa, and handed the passports and papers back to Gregg.

"This is only good for twenty-four hours," the officer instructed. Gregg nodded that he understood, but the officer continued, "You must leave by 11:15 tomorrow morning." Gregg nodded again.

They were several kilometers down the road before

Heather spoke. "This whole country is like one big prison."

"Sure it is."

"How could the people let this happen? I've read the history books, but how did it come to this?"

"I guess everybody just wanted more than everybody else. The thing that tipped it over was when all the truckers went together. Everybody kept striking for more money. Teachers, doctors, garbagemen, auto workers, everybody. The government kept printing paper money trying to keep ahead, but they couldn't. Remember the riots in New York City?"

"Yes," Heather answered. "That was when I was in Grade 13. We talked about it in class. The *Star* and the *Globe and Mail* both had stories about it."

"Then the truckers went together, every trucker in the United States. The Teamsters, the Post Office, ambulance drivers, independents—there wasn't a thing moving in the whole country."

"Who took over? The Army?"

"Not at first. A bunch of Senators, I think it was seven or eight, got together and decided to do something about the crisis. They went to the President and pressured him into declaring a national emergency and calling out the Army to get things rolling again."

"But there's no President now, is there?"

"No. There was so much trouble he had to resign. But by that time the military was running the country, and still is."

"It seems unbelievable." Her voice was low and sad.

"I'm just glad I was already in Toronto."

"Me too, Gregg." He grabbed for a hug, but she pulled away. "Better drive, love." Then, "Gregg, do you think it will ever go back?"

"No. It will never be like it was."

Shaking her head as if she could not believe what she was saying, Heather measured her words, "So now we're down here smuggling Bibles."

Saturday afternoon, December 22

The white wagon took only ten minutes to pass through the crossing point on the Pennsylvania-Ohio border. As Gregg moved away from the barrier, a metallic green Chrysler slipped into the line of traffic two cars behind them, unnoticed. Only the squat radials and a thin antenna stub hinted that this was no family car. Even these gave no hint of the powerful engine under the hood or the heavy duty suspension.

I-90 cut through open farmland here, two gray lines drawn across a world of white, broken here and there by a stand of snow-laden trees. An occasional house or barn interrupted the desolate monotony. In spite of the uninspiring scenery, Heather kept looking at the passing countryside with the fascination of a first-time tourist.

An hour west, a green and yellow sign led Gregg to the Ameriday Inn. Their hostess took them to a booth in the center of the restaurant, while outside, a dark green Chrysler filled up with gas at the service station.

Dark paneling, heavy drapes, red vinyl seats and trim turned the room into an armchair traveler's idea of a castle. A fake coat of arms and two plastic swords completed the picture. Heather had not yet completed her survey of the room before the waitress came, carrying a steaming pot.

"Coffee?"

"One coffee, one tea please," Gregg answered. "And two Ohio Staters. Do you still have that good house dressing, the red stuff?"

"Sounds like you've been here before."

"Yes . . . yes, I have." Gregg wondered now if he had been foolish in stopping here. The fewer patterns in his travels, the better.

Heather hadn't forgotten her earlier lesson. She worked her way through her salad and roast beef sandwich, hacking away with her fork like an American.

Back on I-90, Gregg traveled only a short stretch before turning south on Route 11. After a few kilometers, Heather slipped off her boots, tilted her seat back, and let the motor's rhythm sing her to sleep.

Just north of Youngstown it started snowing again. The wiper's noise brought Heather out of her light doze.

"Hungry?" Gregg asked.

"Not really. Are you?"

"No, but we ought to stop. We need to kill about an hour. I don't want to get there before dark."

"When do we take the Bibles out?" she asked.

"That's another reason I want to wait till dark. We'll get off at the next exit and get a bite."

Belmont Street offered a mixed menu ranging from hamburgers and steaks to chicken or pizza, plus gasoline stations and a discount house. The old cemetery bordering the right-hand side of the road seemed out of place in this plastic wilderness. Gregg turned in at the Big Boy.

Several cars back, two men in the green car saw the Volvo turn off. Quickly the Chrysler cut down a side street, turned around, and came back to pull in at a hamburger house facing the main road. The pair sat in their car and ate, watching the road and talking. They almost missed the Volvo heading out toward Route 11 and I-76.

Gregg paid little attention to the snow-covered car in the parking lot, though he did happen to see someone sitting behind the wheel and, taking another look in his rear view mirror, saw the green car start up as if it were going to come out onto Belmont. But Gregg had to find the right Interstate ramp, and he forgot about the Chrysler.

Gregg followed the highway westward until Route 11 again turned south. Route 11 was four-lane, too, but traffic was lighter and snow was beginning to build up on the road. Gregg could feel the uncertain surface beneath the wheels. The wind came at them broadside, buffeting their wagon and forcing Gregg to make constant slight corrections with the steering wheel.

"How much farther, love?" Gregg recognized anxiety in his wife's question.

"No problem. This car was made in snow country."

"Uh, oh," Gregg gasped moments later.

Then Heather saw it. Two police cruisers on the other side of the median had an old man and woman spread-eagled against the side of their car.

"What do you figure that was about?" Heather asked, looking back and trying to see.

"I don't know."

"Gregg . . . " They both fell into silence.

The storm seemed to change direction with nightfall. Now Gregg's headlights seemed to aim into the very heart of the blast. A million tiny missiles leaped from the blackness to hurl themselves against or around the windshield.

All his senses alert, Gregg coaxed the car to follow the highway. He could almost hear his heart pound above the engine. Beside him Heather sat still and silent. Frequent checks in the mirror told Gregg that someone was following them.

Heather broke the silence. "What's wrong, love?"

"Nothing," he answered, a shade louder than he meant to.

"Is someone following?"

"Of course not."

She turned and looked back, but could see only two dim points of light in the moving blanket behind them. She flipped on the rear window wiper, but could still see only those two faint pinpoints.

"Nobody's following us," Gregg began, as much to reassure himself as Heather. "They couldn't be. That guy is probably letting me break the way."

Ahead of them a huge truck bored through the night, its driver apparently unbothered by the weather. Twin headlights pierced the whiteness like powerful lasers. The flatbed trailer sagged and swayed under two mountains of coiled steel shrouded in flapping tarpaulins.

Eighteen overloaded tires pressed the snow-packed surface and flung bits of grit and ice in every direction, severely limiting visibility for those in the Volvo.

"Pass him, Gregg," urged Heather.

He gripped the wheel harder, fighting the gusts created by the truck and trying desperately to see past the swirling chaos pouring over the windshield. Just then he saw a sign, REST AREA FIVE KILOMETERS. Thinking quickly, he glanced down at the odometer. At just the right moment he took his foot off the gas pedal, watching the rear view mirror. The lights grew brighter, then abruptly receded.

Now. Hoping the tires would hold, Gregg floored the accelerator and swung out into the left lane. Mercilessly he forced the wagon into the noise and shock and blinding gale raised by the truck. Heather shrank away from the tarpaulin's reaching fingers as they passed. Then the Volvo broke clear.

Gregg swerved to the right just in front of the truck—inches from its bumper—and off the road onto the rest area ramp at 120 k's. Quickly he doused the lights and worked the hand brake to slow the car to a crawl.

As the trucker swept past he blew a derisive blast on the horn, which did nothing to warn the dark green sedan now attempting to pass that its quarry had escaped.

Near the far end of the parking area Gregg finally brought the car to a stop and shut off the motor. The only sound was the sigh of wind and snow against the sides and roof of the car.

"Keep a good lookout, Heather. Let me know if anybody turns in here."

Heather turned in her seat to watch the way they had come. "Our tracks are almost covered already."

"Fine."

Outside, Gregg had the rear door open and was reaching in to fold the seat cushion forward.

"How can I help? Do you want the light on?"

"You just keep your eyes on the road," he snapped, "and leave the light off. I can see well enough."

Hurriedly Gregg removed six fasteners from the top edge of the turned up seat cushion. Heather gasped in surprise when he opened the bottom to reveal hundreds of small black books tightly stacked in narrow compartments separated by thin wood frames cut to exact size.

"Watch the road," he reprimanded her.

Gregg emptied two rows and stacked the books in a brown paper grocery sack. Checking to be sure none of the others were loose, he closed the cover and began replacing the fasteners.

Finished, he picked up the sackful of Bibles and handed them up to Heather. The whole operation had taken less than three minutes.

"Ready to go?"

Heather's voice was barely audible. "Gregg, before we go let's have a prayer."

Ashamed, he softened abruptly. "You're right. We've got time for that."

Moments later they were on the road again.

The green car rocketed madly down the highway, far too fast for conditions.

"You fool," the man on the right shouted at the driver, "you lost him. You let him get away."

The driver protested, "He got ahead of us, that's all. We'll catch him."

"Idiot. It's your fault," the other man kept saying. "You lost him when he went around that rig. Then you had to slow up and look for tracks back there at the exit. I say we should have turned off."

"Shut up. I don't care what you say, I say he's still on this road."

"We'd better send out a description," began the passenger, reaching for the hand microphone.

"You leave that alone," the driver screamed. "You want to go on barracks duty again? Not me. We'll find him."

Rebuffed, the second man replaced the mike. "Okay, we look for him. But I say one hour, that's all. If we don't come up with him in one hour, we'll send out an all-points."

"We'll have him in less than an hour."

Saturday night, December 22

"Where do we go, love?"

"The other end of town," he explained. "Look for an old Methodist church. Then we go left."

"How do you remember everything?"

"Just have to. I don't want anything written down."

"What is Citizen's Day?" she asked, seeing a sign in a store window.

"That's Christmas down here. Citizen's Day, when everybody can celebrate their blessings. They couldn't keep people from having the holiday, so they made a new one of their own."

Millburg lay under a snowy blanket. Most of the storefronts were dark. A lone taxi waited by the curb. Plumes of windblown snow swept down from the rooftops and across the deserted street.

Gregg spotted the church and turned left. Heather shuddered at the boarded up doorway and broken windows. Snow gusted through the hole where the rose window had been.

Gregg made a sharp right between two houses and stopped halfway beneath an enormous snow-weighted evergreen. Heather had to get out first, so he could climb out on her side.

"Up this way, I think," he said, carrying the sack. She

followed him up a back stairway, taking a quick look over her shoulder. For a second she froze. What appeared at first to be two hideous eyes was only an old Ford facing them from a shed on the back of the lot. She looked away from the unblinking headlights and hurried up the stairs after Gregg, trying to control her rising panic.

A woman in her fifties answered Gregg's light tap. Heather could barely hear his low salutation.

"Greetings, sister, in the name of Jesus Christ."

The woman's face momentarily clouded before breaking into a wide smile. "Come in. Come in." She stepped back and motioned her visitors inside.

Still talking, she took their coats. "Come in and sit down. John, we have company. Here's one for you, dear. Take the big chair, why don't you. How glad we are to see someone come. Such a bad night, too."

A stoop-shouldered figure entered the room and extended a limp hand. "I'm John Warren and this is my wife, Grace."

"My name's Gregg, and this is Heather."

"The Lord must have sent you to us," Mrs. Warren commented. "We needed company today. Could I get you something hot? I'm sorry I have no coffee, but we can have tea." She started for the kitchen nook just off the living area.

Gregg tried not to notice the worn furniture and bare floors as he spoke to his host. "It's Pastor Warren, isn't it?"

"Yes."

"Friends suggested we drop by and see you. Do you remember Les Johnson?"

"Yes, yes indeed." For an instant the haggard face became alive. "Yes, I remember Les and Kathy. How are they? And the family?"

"Les is fine. They all are, in fact. The girls are still in school. Tracie's eleven, I think, and Christa is eight, and their boy just started school this year."

"Already. It hardly seems possible."

The older man's features took on a weary look as he remembered. From the kitchen Grace could not keep out of the conversation.

"Wasn't she a Fraser?"

Gregg was the one who answered. "That could have been her name. I'm not sure."

Mrs. Warren filled in the data.

"You didn't know them before they were married? She was a girl in our first church. Such a good family, too. She and Les were a perfect pair. John married them."

She came into the living room bearing a tray with cookies and teapot and four exquisite cups and saucers.

"Oh, how lovely." Heather was unaware of the surprise in her voice.

"Those are from the old days. My John used to have the biggest church in the district, and we . . ."

"Grace," her husband interrupted, "don't go into all that."

"It's all right, John," she told him. "These people won't make trouble for us." She turned to her guests. "The hardest time was when John had to give up the church."

Gregg ventured a question. "You're working?"

"Yes," his host answered. "I work in a tank factory. Not military tanks; storage tanks."

"I see."

"After the change I tried to stay on with the church, but it became more and more difficult."

Gregg let him talk, not sure what else to do.

"At first you couldn't tell the difference," Pastor Warren continued, "but gradually our situation altered. Because Social Security listed me as a clergyman, I couldn't have government hospitalization. Separation of church and state, they said. We could have no insurance, no doctor.

"The church tried to take care of us, but it was too much. We couldn't even obtain food coupons. Rather than burden the people, I took the job. I'm a welder's helper. I sweep, do work like that."

"So now you're on the approved list?" Gregg asked.

"That is correct. Now I can enjoy the benefits of social democracy."

"But we're managing," Grace put in quietly, "and the Lord supplies all our needs."

"With some help from the socialists," her husband added.

Gregg looked at his watch. "We must go."

"So soon?" Mrs. Warren queried.

"We wish we could stay longer, but you understand." He glanced at Heather, then back to his host. "Can you use any gifts?"

"Gifts?"

"Bibles," Gregg answered and stepped quickly to the brown sack still sitting by their snow boots.

"Do you actually have Bibles for us?" Pastor Warren asked. "Grace, they have Bibles." He remembered to see if the window blind was down.

"If you'd rather not have them," Gregg began, "we can give them to someone else."

"No." The response was firm. "No. That is, unless you had planned these for others."

"They're yours if you can use them," Gregg told him.

John Warren sighed heavily. "If we can use them! It's a long time since a Bible could be purchased in this country. You don't know what this means. I have eighteen young people, all Christians, and only two of them, only two, have a Bible."

Gregg was by the door, helping Heather with her coat when Mrs. Warren pleaded, "Could you pray with us? Please?"

"Sure we will."

Joining hands, the four made a small circle and offered brief prayers. Heather's cheeks were wet when she reached the car. To think of such a fine Christian pastor being forced out of his church work. . .

"We'll find a motel outside town, after I do something else first," Gregg said.

Driving with his left hand, Gregg reached under the dash. He flipped a switch and instantly the soft music gave way to a cacophony of static and voices. Several minutes farther he stopped the car and extended the radio aerial to its full height.

"Now we'll find out if this thing is worth what we paid for it," he said, back in the car. "We'll let Ian know that we made our first delivery."

"How can you tell him that, love? What if someone hears?"

"I'm merely going to wish him a happy birthday. He'll understand."

Heather tried to make sense out of the jumble of noise coming from the speaker, but it was mostly technical terms and radio talk. "Will it work this far away?" Heather asked.

"It'll work. This is a special job anyway. It'll even get . . ."

". . . Volvo wagon, Ontario license 284-BRX. Repeat, 284-BRX. Car is believed to be heading south into southern Ohio, western Pennsylvania, Kentucky, or West Virginia. Upon sighting, notify Ohio Security Patrol at once. Repeat: This is observation only. Avoid contact."

Gregg drove in silence for several minutes, then once again started tuning across the dial.

"Gregg," Heather pleaded, "you're not going to try to reach him now, are you?"

"We have to try, hon. He'll wonder what happened if I don't. He's praying for us and I want him to know some of the Bibles are already gone."

"Are you going to tell him about the police?"

"I don't know."

"Gregg, I want to go home."

"Hey"—he tried to sound cheerful—"we're okay."

Still tuning across the dial, Gregg came across a round table of several operators. One of the voices was Ian's.

"Gregg, I'm afraid," Heather said, laying her hand on his arm.

"Hon, not now! Please!"

Heather sat back and was still.

Gregg pulled off at a service station closed for the night, turned off the lights, and left the motor running. He groped underneath the center console and brought out a hand microphone. Waiting for the right moment, he increased the speed of the car's engine and pressed the mike button.

"VE3UKH VE3UKH VE3UKH; may I break in?"

Nothing. Only scrambled fragments of a hundred conversations. He tried again.

"VE3UKH VE3UKH VE3UKH; may I break in?"

This time the response was loud and clear.

"Go ahead, breaker; VE3UKH."

"Just wanted to wish you a happy birthday. Happy birthday. Got that, old man?"

More static, but Ian came back immediately.

"Say, I appreciate that. How did you know it was my birthday? I guess I must sound older. Ha. Anything else, breaker? Do you have anything else? Here is VE3UKH standing by."

But Gregg was already out of the car, pushing the antenna down.

Gregg kept his eyes on the road. "We've got to get away from the Warrens. They can't find us this close."

Feeling the back of the car slip on the icy surface, Heather made sure her seat belt was fastened. Driving even faster than usual, Gregg pushed the car into the night.

Sunday morning, December 23

"Hey, sleepyhead," Gregg whispered in his sleeping wife's ear as she dreamed away the early dawn. "Time to get up."

The soft mound of covers outlining her body stirred as she groaned faintly and nestled closer to her husband.

"Hey, come on." Gregg was not to be ignored. "We go to church today, remember?"

Heather half opened her eyes to give her husband a weary smile. "You win, love."

"Did you get any sleep?"

"A little. I hope I didn't keep you awake."

"No. I slept. Don't worry about it, hon. They're not going to do anything to us. We're just down here to visit my folks, and no one's going to do a thing." He kissed her lightly. "I love you. Hey, we better get going."

At breakfast, try as he could Gregg was unable to tell if they were being given special attention by anyone in the dining room. Later, checking out, the desk clerk handed back their passports with routine boredom. Was all as safe and secure as it appeared? Gregg wasn't sure.

Gregg unlocked the car and handed Heather the keys. "You drive."

The look in his eyes squelched Heather's protest, so she started the car while he put their suitcases in back.

"They must not be on to us," Gregg reported.

"You don't think they are watching?"

"Everything is too natural. They don't know about us, not here at least. Let's go. We've got to get some Bibles out."

"Not here, love," Heather cautioned.

"Not here." Gregg pointed to the low roof over the motel dining room, and the closed circuit camera slowly panning the parking area. Seeing the look on Heather's face, he laughed.

"You don't like being on television?"

"Gregg, please."

"I'm sorry."

"What time does the service start?"

"I'm not sure, but we've got lots of time. We're not more than an hour from Central City."

"Is this the large church you were telling me about?"

"This is the big one, the headquarters church for Ohio. They close the smaller churches and force everybody to meet in one big place."

"Tell me if you want to stop," Heather suggested.

"I haven't seen any good place yet. They're all out in the open or too close to people."

Approaching the outskirts of Central City they still had not made the transfer. Ahead they saw a hamburger place and a service station, both closed, but a donut shop open, with customers at the counter. Further on was a discount house, also closed, with the parking lot empty.

"Turn in there." Gregg pointed. "Up along the side."

"Gregg"—her voice was like ice—"I don't think we should."

Then he saw the police car hiding in a drive-in bank entryway. Heather looked straight ahead as they went by, then stiffened as she glanced into the rear view mirror.

"Gregg, he's coming after us."

Without looking around Gregg told her, "Take it easy.

He doesn't have anything on us." *I hope,* he thought.

"What if he follows us?"

"Let him." Gregg cleared his throat.

"What if he follows us to the church?" Heather drove as if she were a student taking a driver's examination.

"We're allowed to attend. It's an open church." Silence, then, "He can't have heard about us over the radio."

"How can you be sure?"

"Because he's too obvious. He knows we see him. He's telling us to watch ourselves while we're in his town."

The police car followed them into the downtown area. Then Gregg had an idea. "Pull over."

She gave him a strange look, then pulled the car to the curb. Gregg jumped out and flagged down the cruiser. Watching the mirror, Heather could see that the officer was giving Gregg directions, with Gregg nodding to show he understood. The police car drove off as Gregg came back to the Volvo.

"Gregg, what did you do?"

"I asked him how to get to the church." Her eyes widened as she listened. "I said we were passing through and wanted to know if there was a church where we could worship. He gave me directions."

"Gregg, you drive now. I don't think I'm up to it."

They traded places and he started the car. Laughing, he told her, "How about that? When you want to find a church in the D.R.A., just ask a cop."

"I don't think it is so funny," she complained.

They found the church building, a red brick box which looked more like a warehouse.

"Why not park in the lot, love?" Heather asked as Gregg wrestled the car in next to the curb. She tensed as a patrol car went by.

"I want to be seen," he told her. "If they're watching us, we'll give them something to look at. I don't want anybody in this car, either. They won't bother it out here."

Inside the plain building the seats were already filling up, though it was still early. A choir loft and baptismal pool lay along the far wall. Organ pipes were symmetrically arranged around a large cross. The pulpit perched on the very front of the choir platform, projecting well out into the audience.

Worshipers kept coming in until every seat was taken. Ushers set up folding chairs in the aisles. Several young people sat on the floor near the organ.

The only sounds in the auditorium were the whispered greetings exchanged between those coming in and those already seated or standing, and the footfalls of latecomers climbing the creaking stairs to the balcony.

Afterward, Heather could not remember much about the service. The organ, the choir, the sermons—both of them—were good, but not outstanding. The service was long. The crowd accounted for that, considering the time it took for Communion. It could have been any service back home. Nothing special. Just a service.

Then it struck her. Christmas had not been mentioned! The first speaker had touched on Christ's birth, but not in depth and had not used the word "Christmas." The second message dealt with self-denial and taking up the cross.

Nearly crushed by the massed crowd slowly flowing toward the exits, Heather looked for Gregg. Over there by the stairs, in conversation with a man and a boy, probably the man's son.

Someone was speaking to her. A woman. Smiling, friendly. "Welcome. We're glad you were here."

"Thank you. I was glad to be here."

"Are you visiting?"

"Yes. From Canada. My husband and I are down on holidays."

"Thank you for coming."

Others, overhearing, whispered greetings and agreement.

"We're glad you've come."

"God bless you, sister."

Someone behind was talking, but Heather, pressed in by the crowd, could not turn to see who it was. "We're thankful when others come. We're so alone now."

Heather stepped out onto the sidewalk, with Gregg just a short way behind. Across the street sat two patrolmen in a police car, watching the congregation leaving the building.

"Looks like we have company," Gregg said, steering her toward the Volvo, careful not to walk too fast. Heather felt as if she were on trial. "Gregg, do you think they're here because of us?"

"I doubt it. They probably come every Sunday. They're probably more regular than some of the members."

"I don't like it."

As he started the car and drove off, he watched the rear view mirror to see if the police car would follow them. It stayed at the church.

"Where are we going?" Heather inquired.

"We're going to pick up a passenger."

"A passenger?" she asked, her voice trembling.

"Keep your eyes open," he told her. "If we see any cops, we keep right on going." Gregg slowed down and looked up each side street and along the buildings. "He should be along here someplace . . . there he is." Heather recognized the boy she had seen at the church.

"We're going to transfer some Bibles, Heather. Nathan is taking us to the place where we are going to meet his father."

Gregg spotted a milk and bread store and pulled into the parking lot.

"Come on, Heather. We'll be right back, Nathan."

She gave Gregg a questioning look, but pulled her coat around her and got out of the car.

Inside, they waited for the customer ahead of them to pay and leave, then Gregg asked for a pound of lunch meat and a half pound of cheese.

While the proprietor was busy with the slicer, Gregg sauntered through the store, picking up buns and corn chips and several bottles of pop. As an afterthought, he went back for six loaves of bread and brought them to the counter.

Heather gave her husband an "I don't understand" look. He just winked at her.

Adding up the total on the cash register, the little man looked as if he wanted to ask a question. "Are you from around here?"

"We're from Canada," Greg answered slowly.

"From Canada?" The man was surprised. "Down here for a visit?" A woman emerged from the back room. The storekeeper's wife, evidently. She must have overheard.

Gregg took his change and picked up his purchases. "Brought my wife down so she could see the sights."

Both the little man and his wife smiled at that and looked at Heather, who explained, "We're on Christmas holidays."

"How nice," the woman said.

Something in her voice prompted Gregg. "Could we, could we wish you a Merry Christmas?"

Taking a deep breath the little man said evenly, "We still have Christmas in our house. Christmas for the real reason." His words hung in the air.

"So do we, my brother. So do we."

The man's face lit up and he looked at his wife, also beaming.

Gregg picked up his purchases, nodded to Heather, and turned to go. Near the door, Heather whispered, "Let's give them a Bible, Gregg." He shook his head and held the door for her.

Their passenger had scooted down in the seat until he was almost on the floor. He didn't sit up until they had gone several blocks. As they drove, Gregg kept looking up and down each side street.

"Twenty minutes," he muttered, intimidated by the dashboard clock, "and we still don't have those Bibles out. I've got it"—Gregg was almost shouting—"That car wash back there."

"Car wash?" Heather was confused.

"Perfect," he said, looking for a place to turn the car around. "Do you have any American quarters?"

She began to rummage through her change purse, still not understanding what her husband was talking about.

"Give them all to Nathan," Gregg told her. "Nathan, how about giving this old buggy a quick rinse?" Looking back and seeing the look on Nathan's face, Gregg added, "I know this is Sunday, but the ox is in the ditch."

"Empty out that stuff," he advised Heather. She began taking things out of the grocery bags and making a little pile by her feet. Finished, she held the two empty grocery sacks in readiness.

At the Quick Wash, Gregg pulled into the self-service bay. "Heather, help me get the seat up and hold it. Can you move your seat forward? Okay, Nathan."

Shielded by the curtain of spray, Gregg moved quickly.

He was finished, sweating but finished, and the seat was back down before the high pressure spray had ended.

Ten minutes later Nathan directed them to a large shopping mall and guided them toward the supermarket at the far end of the parking area. Gregg found what they were looking for: a dark-colored Ford with a vinyl top. There was even an empty space next to it.

"Great," he said, "they're not here yet. Hon, could you put some bread in each sack, so it sticks out at the top?"

Heather had just finished when a couple came out of the supermarket and started across the parking lot, each carrying a sack of groceries.

"Here they come," said Nathan.

Seemingly unaware of the people in the Volvo, Nathan's parents came to their car, opened both back doors, and sat their groceries on the seat. Nathan transferred both sacks to his parents' car in an instant.

"Let's go," Gregg urged Heather. "We're going into the mall. Move."

Without a backward glance the Ford pulled away. No one noticed the two young people walking toward the mall entrance, holding hands and laughing together.

Neither Gregg nor Heather, nor the occupants of the Ford saw the two-man cruiser turn into the shopping center and begin its slow tour of the parking lot.

"Forty-one here," Officer Burke reported into the two-way radio.

"Go ahead, forty-one," came the dispatcher's answer.

"We're at Westgate Mall, and we've spotted the white Volvo wagon listed on today's bulletin from Security."

"One moment, forty-one." A pause. "I've found it. Is that Ontario 284-BRX?"

"Affirmative."

"What's the situation on the car?"

"We made a quick check. The car is locked. Williams looked in and saw nothing but suitcases and groceries and what seems to be a box of motor oil. Some of the groceries are on the floor, but that's the only thing unusual we could see. What's the tag on the car?"

"One moment, forty-one." Another pause. "Looks like a

standard observation order to me. Hold on. I'll get a readout on this. Can you see the car?"

"Affirmative."

Moments later the dispatcher's voice came over the speaker in the patrol car again.

"Burke, you have a teacher and his wife. She's Canadian. He was U. S. and did not change. Frequent visitor. Came over the day before yesterday. Registered in a Buffalo motel Friday. Last night they were in Salem at the Mac-Mar. Seem to be headed south."

"What are they wanted for?"

"The rap sheet doesn't give anything. Security is interested in finding out why he keeps coming back down here."

"You don't want us on that."

"Right, forty-one. Maintain observation and I'll have Keating bring a plain car out there in ten minutes."

Nearer twenty had passed before a sleek tan and gold Firebird swung into the parking area. The young man behind the wheel hardly spared a glance for the police cruiser as he selected a spot two rows behind the Volvo. The two-man car drove off and the driver of the Firebird settled into his seat.

He didn't have long to wait. The girl drew his attention the minute she stepped out of the mall. Keating had her and her escort figured to be his quarry before they reached their car.

He watched as the two of them came closer. The girl kept turning her head and looking up at her husband, laughing, teasing. The Firebird trailed several cars back as the Volvo headed out of town.

Four and a half hours later Detective Keating spoke into a pay telephone in a motel lobby southwest of Central City. He kept looking over his shoulder to be certain no one was eavesdropping.

"They're registered for one night . . . Yes, the Town Crier Inn . . . I'd better get registered, then . . . I don't know. Probably eating supper . . . Yes. Sometime tomorrow. About ten or later."

Keating hung up the phone, disgusted with the prospect

of another night imprisoned in a motel room condemned to government TV. Down the hall, the couple he had followed to the Town Crier had just turned on their set, but they had no intentions of watching it. Not tonight.

Sunday night, December 23

"Let's go," said Gregg, looking again at his watch. "They're probably already started."

Heather took one last look in the mirror. "Aren't you going to turn off the television?"

Gregg shook his head. "Let's leave the light on, too."

He stepped over to the hallway door and listened a moment. Winking at Heather, he opened it and motioned her through. Quickly he followed her out into the hall and hurried her toward the exit. Their footsteps sounded like thunder in the empty hallway.

"So far, so good," Gregg whispered as they stepped out into the frozen night. "This way," he hissed, heading toward the rear of the motel.

The parking lot had been plowed clear of snow, but icy patches made it difficult for Heather to keep her footing as she clung to Gregg's arm. Once they gained the corner, he slowed a bit.

Because of the narrow path through the heavy snow, Heather had to walk behind him. The sidewalks had not been shoveled. Several blocks from their motel, Gregg stopped.

"What is it, love?"

"This is Grant Street," he answered, pointing to the marker. "The church should be real close."

Uncertain which way to go, and not wanting to stay where they were, Gregg turned down the side street. Long rows of old houses crowded close to the sidewalk. Stumbling along behind her husband, Heather had a hard time keeping up.

They hurried two more blocks, neither of them saying a word, before Gregg stopped again. Heather was glad for the rest. "Love," she panted, "please don't walk so fast."

"I'm sorry, hon," he apologized. For a moment he looked around, hesitating. "The church should be right here."

"Gregg, are we lost?"

"Listen."

Far in the distance she could hear the sound of a train engine, played against a faint background of highway noise. Nothing else. Nearby the wind strummed a television antenna. A gate or shutter thumped softly in the wind.

"Listen," Gregg whispered again.

Then she heard it. Singing. A hymn. They tried to pinpoint the direction.

"This way." Gregg took the lead. As they kept walking, the sound grew and then they could see the little frame building halfway down a back street. On the church steps Gregg whispered into his wife's ear, "Remember, we heard the singing and decided to come in." She nodded.

The sudden appearance of two strangers momentarily halted the singing as every eye turned toward the door. The pianist kept bravely on and several stalwarts picked up the beat. Gradually the singing resumed, though with less spirit than before.

A dignified older gentleman rose and came toward them, extending his hand to Gregg.

"We're passing through," Gregg whispered before his host could speak, "and we wanted to find a place of worship tonight."

"You're welcome here," the older man responded. "Will you sing with us?"

He invited them to follow and offered them a place next to his prim wife, starched and proper. She handed Heather a songbook. Heather took the worn hymnal, and she and Gregg joined in the song.

Gregg counted thirty-seven people in the congregation, including a handful of young people and two small children. Trying not to be obvious, he surveyed the small chapel, taking note of the room's new paint and bright appearance.

Except for damp footprints, the aisle runner was spotless, and the hardwood floor fairly shone under the freshly scrubbed pews.

In spite of the leader's genuine welcome and the warm atmosphere of the building, there was an electric tension in the room. The songleader announced the next hymn in a timorous voice, his manner taut and strained. The music began again, almost mechanically.

Suddenly Gregg became aware that the man next to him and the people in front were listening to his singing. He stole a glance at Heather and saw that she, too, realized they were on display.

The strain relaxed somewhat when prayer time came. Most kept their petitions short. Gregg joined in with the "Amens" at the close.

A sandy-haired young man in his twenties rose and turned to face the audience. "Tonight we will continue our study of Matthew. If you'll turn to chapter six, we will examine Jesus' attitude toward giving and look at His teaching on prayer."

He caught his breath, then continued. "We're glad to have visitors tonight. We want you to know you are welcome here, and we hope you will visit with us again."

Gregg started to reply, waiting for the speaker to give him the opportunity, but the expected pause never came. Instead, the leader went directly into his lesson.

He had to see I wanted to say something, Gregg thought to himself. *He had to see. I wonder why he didn't let me speak.*

The leader never did stop. His lecture completely barred any response from the congregation, and when he was finished he expressed the benediction himself.

Afterward the little band of believers crowded around their two guests, shaking hands, expressing greetings, and asking questions.

"We're friends from Toronto."

"Welcome. So happy you came."

"Thank you."

"How did you find us?"

"We were walking and heard the singing."

"We'll have to watch out if we're singing that loudly."

"We bring greetings from the church in Canada."

"Yes; thank you. Take our greetings back to them."

Finally the little group dispersed, all except the young man who had given the lesson. While others had been talking he had busied himself around the front of the building, straightening chairs and replacing hymnals in the racks. Now he came to meet his guests.

"So glad you've come. Are you from around here?"

"No," answered Gregg. "We're from Toronto. We're just passing through."

A moment's hesitation, then, "Would you happen to know any MacFarlands?"

"I knew it," Gregg said. "You must be Don Donaldson. I bring a special hello for you from Scott and Mary and the family."

"Scott and Mary," he repeated, almost reverently. "How are they? It seems like it's been so long."

"They're both well. The girls, too."

A shadow crossed Don's face. When the question came, it was only one word: "Angela?"

Had Gregg not already known, the look on Don's face would have explained the question. Gregg tried to answer as gently as he could.

"Angela married about a year ago. She married a fellow from the Willowdale Church. I believe they're expecting some time in the spring."

Don turned away, saying something about turning off the lights. "Angela asked me to send you a special greeting from her, Don."

Don turned back, eyes brimming, and said huskily, "We tried. We really tried. But there was no way . . . The border."

Gregg nodded his head in understanding as Don continued. "Can you come to my place? You don't have to go yet, do you?"

"We could stay a few minutes." Gregg glanced around to be sure no one else was there. "We have a few Bibles, too, if you can use them."

Don took Gregg's hand and gripped it tightly. "Let's go."

His basement apartment was small, but adequate. "This is home," Don said, "and you're welcome. I'm sorry I couldn't ask you to bring greetings or speak in the service."

"I understand," Gregg said.

"Tell me about your church. Where do you attend?"

"We meet in a mall," Gregg began. His host registered surprise. "The Sheridan Mall. Have you ever been to Toronto?"

"No." Don shook his head. "I've seen pictures. Angela sent me some right after they crossed."

Gregg turned the subject back to the church. "Downstairs they have a big area which can be divided off into different rooms. We use the whole thing."

"How many attend?"

"About 220, 250."

"Is your church growing?"

Heather spoke up. "From all that Gregg has told me, we Canadians must be a bit more hesitant than Americans, or than Americans used to be, and our churches do not grow very rapidly. But our church is reaching new families and we're seeing people come to Jesus."

"You're not from Canada?" Don asked Gregg.

"No. My dad was transferred up, then transferred back, but by then I was in university and when the change came I stayed." Gregg remembered why he was there. "Don, could we leave you a few Bibles?"

Don shot a glance at the ground level window above Heather's chair. "Friend, I can take as many as you can leave with me."

Gregg looked at Heather, and she opened her purse and emptied out a dozen small Bibles. With what Gregg had in his coat pockets, there were twenty in two neat stacks on the coffee table.

"We must go, Don," Gregg began. "Could we pray together before we separate?"

"I'd like to," Don said. He had a question he was hesitant to ask, but found the words. "Would you . . . do you have a lot of Bibles? What I am asking is, would you be able to stop and see a family and leave a few with them? That is, if you are going that way."

"Where do they live?"

"Down along the river. Southeast of here about eighty kilometers."

"Still in Ohio?"

"Yes."

"Sure. We could do that."

Don left the room and returned with a sheet of paper. He drew a map for Gregg. Then the three of them formed a small circle around the little black books on the coffee table.

Back at the Town Crier, Keating had had enough. He used his fist on the TV "off" button, turned off the lights, and went down the hall toward the lounge.

Passing Room 126 he hesitated, listened to the sounds coming through the door, and kept going. Had they come straight to 126, Gregg and Heather would have met Keating in the hallway. Instead, Gregg had led Heather toward the car.

"Are you going to wish Ian happy birthday again?" Heather asked.

"No, but I'll tell him something."

"You're not going to try and contact him from here?"

"No. We'll drive to some high place and . . ." He stopped in his tracks and grabbed her arm.

"What is it?"

"Wait," he whispered. Moving slowly to the corner of the building, Gregg carefully took another look. Quickly he urged Heather back the way they had come.

"Police," he whispered.

"Oh, Gregg," she gasped, "are they after us?"

"No." He sounded more sure than he felt.

"What if they are, Gregg?"

He ignored her.

"Wait." He stopped her at the door to their hallway and checked to see whether anyone could be seen.

"There's no one," he told Heather, adding, "Come on. We've got to get in that room."

Monday morning, December 24

Standing in the motel foyer, Heather stifled a yawn as she waited for Gregg to check out. She had slept poorly, again.

The desk clerk found their bill and began adding up the charges. Behind him a huge poster dominated the wall, its black lettering on a red background announcing DEMOCRACY—EQUALITY—FREEDOM. Heather shuddered. She wanted to scream.

"Any phone calls?" the clerk asked.

"No."

"Dining room charges?"

"Only the breakfast, and our dinner last night."

"I have those."

While the clerk added up the figures, Gregg took a pencil from the desk and started doodling on a scratch pad lying on the counter, making a shallow arc, tracing the design back and forth several times.

"Thank you for staying with us," said the clerk, handing Gregg his change and the two passports.

"Where do we go today, love," Heather asked, once they were in the car.

"Today we're going to pick up 3,000 dollars."

"We are going to do what?"

Gregg picked his way through the morning traffic, checking his mirror now and then. "We're going to pick up 3,000 dollars," he repeated.

"Gregg, are you teasing me?"

"No, I'm not," he told her. "And we're going to deliver a few Bibles to those people Don told us about. By the way, we would do well to find a place to stop and get some more out."

"What about the money?" she wanted to know.

"You remember Joe Stevens? The fellow I told you about from Hamilton? He came down here a couple of years ago and had 3,000 dollars for families of prisoners. Preachers' families mostly."

"But wasn't he sent to prison?"

"He's the one. Anyway, Stevens came down with this money. He had some names, too. Stevens found out government men were following him and stashed the money in his motel room. We're going to stay at that same motel tonight, if we can."

"Gregg, this really scares me."

"We're not going to get caught." *Help us, Lord,* he prayed silently.

They headed south on a two-lane highway marked with faded signs boasting SCENIC ROUTE.

"Gregg, you didn't tell me we were going to do things like this."

"Look, hon." His voice was firm. "I didn't tell you because I didn't want you to start worrying. Relax. Nothing's going to happen to us."

She sank back in her seat. "Did they search Mr. Stevens? Did they catch him?"

Gregg nodded reluctantly.

Heather was afraid to ask for more information, but she had to know. "What happened to him?"

"They put him in jail for six months."

"Six months? What did they accuse him of doing?"

"They charged him with currency speculation."

"Oh," she said, relieved. "What exactly was he doing?"

Gregg wished he could just let the subject drop, but the look in his wife's eyes told him he had to tell her the truth. "He had about a hundred Bibles when they caught him."

Heather almost screamed. "A hundred? Gregg, we have . . ." She closed her eyes and laid her head against the headrest. Gregg kept talking; there was no reason to keep anything from her now.

"They charged him with currency speculation because each Bible is worth probably seventy-five or 100 dollars. If we'd sell them, that is."

Heather put her hand over her face. "So then we're carrying . . . Oh, love, we will never . . ." Her voice trailed off.

He reached over and took her hand. "Look, hon, we're not going to get into trouble. I just want to do as much as we can this time. There's such a need, such a need."

"Gregg, what will we do with the money?"

"Give it to a woman whose husband is in prison."

She put her hand over her mouth. "I think I'm going to bring up."

He shut off the heater. "Roll the window down. The cold air will make you feel better. And don't worry, hon. If it looks too bad . . . well, we'll wait and see."

She didn't answer, but laid her head against the door frame and let the cold air blow against her forehead. She wanted to serve Christ, but this . . . this . . .

Shortly before noon they reached Riverton, a grimy collection of smokestacks rising out of dirty snow.

"No pollution control here," Gregg muttered as they splashed through the filthy slush behind a coal truck.

"What happens if we don't find the right people?" She felt a little better now.

"We'll find them. Don drew a good map."

Gregg's confidence proved well-founded. He had no trouble finding the address, a gray shingled two-story cut up into several apartments. Gregg walked up the front steps carrying two grocery sacks, loaves of bread sticking out of each bag.

Inside the narrow hallway Gregg inspected the row of mailboxes. *J. T. Johnson. Apt. 5.* In two strides Gregg was on the landing. Three more and he was upstairs in the corridor, tapping at the door.

No answer. He knocked again, louder. Sounds of people carried to him from behind the doors, but which one? He couldn't be sure. But he was sure of one thing—in each door was a peephole and he had the strong feeling he was being watched.

Gregg hesitated before knocking again, but finally tapped on the door of the Johnson apartment. Involuntarily, Gregg shivered. These apartment hallways must be unheated.

No answer. Nothing to do but leave.

"What do we do now?" Heather asked as they drove away.

"Get a snack somewhere and kill some time."

"We could take some photographs," she suggested. "I don't have very many yet."

"My wife the picture hunter," he chided her. "Besides, you'll freeze."

"We *don't* have many pictures, love. And you said we would take some. Is there anything in the area we could see?"

"We ought to be able to find some old buildings."

"Let's try and find something."

Riverton offered few opportunities for good photographs. A friendly gasoline attendant directed them to an old log structure, originally a land office. Gregg stomped around in the snow while Heather made a few quick sketches on her drawing pad. After he had taken several pictures, he came back and looked over her shoulder.

He never ceased to be amazed at Heather's ability to create an image on paper or canvas. She had to quit after only a few minutes because her ungloved hand could not stand the wind.

Instead of going back the way they had come, Gregg wheeled the car down a steep valley. "Let's go take a look at the ice on the river and . . ." He didn't finish the sentence. "Well, would you look who's here."

Tucked into a narrow space between two buildings sat a tan Firebird, its driver just getting into the car. Gregg couldn't resist a wave as they went past. At the bottom of the hill he turned toward downtown.

"They're really clumsy if this is the best they've got," he fumed. Heather remained silent, staring straight ahead.

"Gregg"—her voice carried a metallic quality—"he knows about us."

"No way."

One of the mills must have changed shifts. Traffic was getting heavy.

"That guy was just keeping an eye on us."

Gregg waited impatiently for a traffic signal to change. Heather saw him check the mirror again. "Is he back there?"

"No. I don't see him." The light changed. "He won't be either. He'll call for someone else, now that he knows we're on to him."

Gregg suddenly swerved down a narrow side street, then braked and cut sharply into an alley. Pools of slush between brick-hard stretches of ice had transformed the alley into a proving ground. Gregg pounded the Volvo over the uneven roadbed, sliding to a stop at each street crossing, accelerating as much as he dared in between.

"Where are we going now?"

"Back to the Johnsons'." Heather started to protest, but he didn't give her a chance. "If I figure it right, we've got ten minutes."

"Ten minutes?"

He explained, "Before they can get another car on to us. They'll have to find us first."

"What if"—she braced herself with her left hand against the dashboard and her right hand gripping the door armrest—"what if he was following when we stopped there before?"

Gregg let up on the accelerator. "I never thought of that. You're right."

She caught her breath. "We should not go back, should we?"

"No. We can't take the chance of getting them in trouble."

"Us too, love."

"Okay. Us too." He grinned at her.

He drove aimlessly for several minutes until they came to a main highway. Looking at the sign, he turned westward, then remembered something else. "I'd like to check in with Ian tonight. He'll be wondering about us."

Heather felt a rising surge of tension. "Love, please, let's not use the radio. Not tonight."

Gregg reached across and laid his arm on her shoulder, then teased her hair with his fingertips.

"Hey," he said with forced cheer, "we're going to be fine. Tell you what, tonight we don't use the short wave. How's that?"

To give her something to do, he suggested, "Let's have some music, at least. See if you can get CFRB this time of day."

Heather leaned forward and moved the pointer back and forth in the right range, but the Canadian station eluded her.

"Can't in the daytime, I guess," said Gregg. "Maybe after dark."

Heather rotated the adjustment knob and tilted her seat about twenty degrees. She leaned back and closed her eyes. "Love, I don't know if I can take being married to you. I am beginning to feel old already, and we haven't been married six months."

Gregg laughed. "Just think what it will be like after fifty years. You haven't seen anything yet."

She could only groan.

Standing in the phone booth, Officer Keating shifted from one foot to the other as he reported to his superior, Captain Lawrence Callihan.

"Sir, I think we are following two newlyweds on a honeymoon trip over the holidays."

"You've been with them since Central City?"

"Yes, sir."

"Followed them all that time?"

"Yes, sir."

"They've not been out of your sight?" Demanding, this Callihan.

"No, sir. That is, not for long."

"What do you mean?"

"Well, sir, I must have missed a turn at Riverton. I was sitting on top of him, then he was gone. I kept on into town and waited at a gas station and picked him up again."

"How long was he out of your sight?"

"Not more than ten or twelve minutes. Maybe fifteen."

"Then he spotted you?"

"No, sir. Not then. They were taking pictures at this old log house. I had parked on a side street. When they started up from taking the pictures he came around and down my street."

"You're sure he did not see you?"

"No, sir. Not until then. I think he was taking a shortcut."

Callihan's voice revealed his skepticism. "A shortcut?"

"Yes, sir. To the downtown section. I should have thought of that possibility, but it never occurred to me."

"So he saw you." Even over the phone, Callihan's scorn came through.

Keating's reply was a subdued, "Yes, sir."

"And you think he knows you were following him?"

"Sir, I have no way of knowing. But he couldn't help getting a good look at me and the car. And if he sees me again, he'll know for sure."

"So now you're suggesting we call this whole thing off?"

Keating had to clear his throat. "Yes, sir."

"Do you know who put out this observation order?"

"Security?"

"Go to the head of your class." Keating could hear the rattle of paper as his commanding officer kept talking. "I have here in my hot little hands a memo sent out to underlings such as you and me. In case you don't know what I am talking about, this is an observation order. An observation order, Keating, for Ontario Volvo 284-BRX. I wouldn't be surprised if this piece of paper came from Wilson himself."

Keating could only reply, "Yes, sir."

He could hear what sounded like Captain Callihan's chair scraping against the floor. Keating winced as his superior's voice shouted at him over the phone.

"And you want me to call down there and tell them we're on a wild goose chase?"

Keating didn't back down. "Sir, I believe we're following a pair of nobodies. I am only suggesting that we, or you, or someone file a report suggesting that we see no need for continued surveillance."

Keating thought the connection had been broken. Callihan finally spoke. "Keating, you had better not be wrong. Your suggestion will go into my daily report when I send it tonight, and I am taking you off this assignment as of now."

"Yes, sir."

"Turn in your log tomorrow. No need to bring it in tonight. You'll get back late enough as it is."

"Sir, tomorrow is the holiday."

"So it is, Keating. To show you I'm not all bad, I'll give you the day off."

Situated about a third of the way up a small hill locally termed a mountain, The Stone Lodge had the appearance of a secure refuge from the rigors of the highway.

A long driveway gently curved between two rows of snow-trimmed pines, the trees skillfully illuminated by miniature floodlights half buried in the snow. Two wings branched out on either side of the lobby, restaurant, and pool area. An A-frame, the old lodge looked like an enormous mountain retreat.

"Peaceful, isn't it?" Gregg observed as they followed the driveway to the office.

"Quiet, too," Heather agreed. "Did you make a reservation?"

"No, but I don't think we'll have any trouble, even with the celebrating. My thinking is that they'll all go home afterwards. For the most part, anyway."

"I'll stay in the car, love, if you don't mind."

"Sure." Gregg checked to see that he had both passports, then left. He came back in a few minutes all smiles, merrily jingling the key at arm's length.

"What are you so happy about?" Heather asked as he got back into the car and drove down to the wing where they were staying.

"I didn't get *the* room, but we're across the hall."

Now Heather remembered. A wave of fear engulfed her. Oblivious to his wife's apprehension, Gregg kept talking. "I was afraid to ask for 221, but we're close; 230. There's a big party going on tonight, so I asked if we could be on the second floor, away from the noise."

Inside, The Stone Lodge was as elaborate as on the outside. Entering the reception area was like entering a

54 CHECKPOINT

cathedral, the massive floor to ceiling timbers meeting far overhead, at once inviting the eyes upward. A large balcony served as a meeting point for the second floor hallways coming from each wing and feeding into the open end of the dining room.

The reception desk sat completely out in the open, and two bright young women in matching pantsuits worked behind a low marble-topped table, greeting incoming guests and tending to the room assignments. Gregg counted three security guards: one by the far hallway, one visible on the upstairs balcony, and one by the front door.

Heather sidled up to Gregg. "How much are we paying for this place?"

"It's Christmas Eve," he whispered. "Remember?"

A bellboy carried their things up to Room 230. Gregg fumbled in his billfold, wondering how much was enough, but the boy left before Gregg had time to give him anything.

Gregg suggested, "Let's celebrate. Put on something nice."

Heather perked up. "Should I wear my green dress?"

"Perfect!"

"I won't take but a minute," she said, slipping into the bathroom to freshen up and change. Gregg flipped off the lights and stepped over to the window. He parted the drapes just barely so that he had a narrow slit through which to survey the parking lot. From up here the driveway and the snow-covered hillside were even more beautiful. The tranquil setting contrasted sharply with Gregg's inner feelings.

"Lord," he prayed aloud, his voice low so Heather could not hear, "you've got to help us tonight."

Gregg looked down at the cars on the lot and wondered which one belonged to their pursuers.

"Dear God, You know whether they are on to us. You know how much Your children need that money. And You know what the police will do to us if they catch us."

Gregg backed away from the window and raised his hands toward the ceiling.

"I can't do it myself, Lord. I can't. You know if the

money is even there, and You know if we can get it out of
that room. Oh God, God"—Gregg clenched his fists—
"help us tonight. Thank You for bringing us this far. Thank
You for the border crossings. Thank You for Heather.
Lord, don't let anything happen to her, don't let anything
. . ."

When the bathroom door suddenly opened, Gregg relaxed
and turned around casually. Grinning, he turned on the
lights and pulled at the drapes. The cords were broken and
he had to close them by hand. Looking his wife up and
down, he announced, "Tonight I have a date with the most
beautiful girl in the D.R.A."

The dining room occupied the second floor of the
A-frame. Since there was no third story, the ceiling soared
over the tables and chairs. Floor to ceiling stonework
formed the back wall, framing an enormous fireplace. A
large blue spruce stood to one side, beautifully decorated,
the ornaments glinting back the reflected fire on the hearth.
To the right stood a bandstand.

Each table was decorated with a red candle ringed with
plastic holly. The flickering candles and the lighted tree
made the chilly room seem smaller, warmer.

"A year ago tonight," Gregg reminisced, "I asked you to
become my wife."

"And I accepted your invitation."

Their salads came and Heather instinctively bowed her
head, then stopped herself. She looked up at Gregg.

"Hard not to, isn't it?" he whispered.

She nodded. Not thinking, she reached for her knife and
fork, Canadian style, and caught herself again. Gregg
winked at her.

"Still thinking about last year?" Gregg asked.

"When you gave me that book I was so disappointed."

"Hey, it took a lot of work to cut out all those pages."

"What was the name of it? I've forgotten."

"*The Saint Meets His Match.* Appropriate, don't you
think? A good old Les Charteris thriller. I read it before I
cut out the place for the ring."

"Remember our dinner at home afterward?"

"And the dessert?" Gregg's teasing made them both burst

out laughing. Others were turning to look, so they toned down their exuberance.

"You sure did squirt me with that whipped cream." Gregg ducked as though he was being squirted now.

"I was so embarrassed. All over your face and your shirt."

Suddenly Heather froze, then tried to look unconcerned again. Gregg stopped laughing. "What's the matter?"

"Nothing. A security man just came in, that's all."

"Let him." Heather saw something else which made her start. "Now what is it?" Gregg asked her.

"Gregg"—the laughter was gone out of her voice—"there's a man over there staring right at us. He's watching us. I know he is."

Leaning closer over the heat of the candle, he told her in a near whisper, "Next time I'm not going to marry such a good-looking wife."

Her cheeks colored again. "You're impossible." She couldn't stay afraid, not with Gregg's constant banter.

At the cash register Gregg made a quarter moon under his signature on the back of their dinner check. It went unnoticed by the cashier.

As they passed Room 221, Gregg stopped and leaned close to the door. Heather stiffened with fear, but he straightened up and gave her an "I don't know" look. They kept walking down the hall.

Inside their own room, Gregg secured the door locks and went over to inspect their luggage.

Heather whispered, "Has it been bothered?"

"No."

"What do we do now, love?"

He checked his watch. "I figure we've got an hour, maybe an hour and a half." He looked around the room, taking an elaborate survey of the ceiling, the drapes, the desk and chair and the bed. His gaze came to rest on his wife as he said softly, "Must be something we can do."

She started to reply, but he was suddenly digging into the big suitcase. He brought out one of his socks, its limp form concealing a box about eight inches long, wrapped in Christmas foil.

Surprised, Heather accepted the gift and laid it on the bed, then went over to her purse and took out a package of her own.

"How did you keep me from knowing this?" she asked as her fingers stripped away the expensive wrapping. She opened the lid to reveal a set of artist's brushes and a palette knife.

"Oh, Gregg," she exclaimed. "They're just what I need."

Impulsively she threw herself at him and hugged him, then abruptly pushed herself away.

"Unwrap yours," she suggested.

Gregg made no move toward the package. "Hon," he asked, a catch in his voice, "do you have any idea how much I love you?"

Her eyes met his and she stood still, a study in flawless, living marble. Without taking her eyes away from him, she slipped off one shoe, then the other.

"Oh, Gregg," she kept saying as she clung to him. "Gregg, Gregg, my darling."

"Merry Christmas," he whispered as her lips sought his.

Late Monday night, December 24

Gregg looked again at his watch, the third time in less than two minutes. "About ready?"

Nearly finished with her hair, Heather patted the last few strands into place. She laid the brush on the table and turned to face him. "Love, I don't think I can do this."

Gregg got out of the chair and put his arms around her. "Hon," he whispered in her ear, "you can. We'll be all right. Nothing will happen, I promise, and I need you to help me."

He put his hand under her chin and tried to get her to look at him, but she buried her face in his shoulder and started to sob. "Gregg"—her voice was muffled—"I'm so afraid."

This time he succeeded in turning her face so he could

look at her. Her cheeks were wet, but she had stopped crying. Her lower lip trembled. He gave her a soft kiss and brushed a tear away with his hand.

Looking at Heather, tracing the familiar loveliness of her cheekbones and throat, touching the baby curls on the back of her neck, Gregg felt an overwhelming longing to call the whole thing off, but he couldn't—he had to go on. One word was all he could manage.

"Ready?"

"If you are." She reached for a tissue and dabbed at her eyes.

"Let's pray first."

In the silence, the sounds from the party on the first floor carried to them. Gregg got down on his knees, then Heather knelt beside him. After they were finished he helped her up. Quickly he went over his last-minute instructions.

"When we get in there, you stay by the door and keep your ears open. That money should be somewhere behind the heater. I'll work as fast as I can, but you've got to listen for anybody coming."

He checked his pockets again: screwdriver, pliers, socket and wrench. On two practice runs with their own heater unit, Heather had timed him at six minutes flat to take the cover off, put it back on, and tighten the screws.

Gregg put the tools back in his pocket. In his left hand he held a thin piece of steel about five inches long and half an inch wide. They were as ready as they would ever be.

He looked again at Heather. "Do you have our room key?"

"Yes."

He opened their door and stepped into the hallway. Down at the other end a man was disappearing into the far stairwell, so Gregg fiddled with their doorknob as if he were making sure it was locked, until the man was gone.

In seconds Gregg was at the door of Room 221. Quickly he inserted the metal strip between the door and the molding. The tolerance on this door was much closer than on the room he and Heather were staying in. This would not be easy.

Gregg's instrument kept butting against the door jamb—

there was just not enough room to force the thin strip around the corner to put pressure on the lock. Worse, he had never given a thought to gloves. A stab of pain and the spread of crimson across his palm reproached his carelessness. Gregg hurriedly wrapped his handkerchief around his hand.

"Oh, love," Heather exclaimed softly. She leaned over and tried to see how badly he was hurt.

"It's okay," he hissed and bent to work on the door again. Sudden voices and the snap of a latch brought both of them to instant attention. People were coming out of a room down the hall.

Gregg crammed his bandaged hand into his pants pocket, grabbed Heather's arm, and in an instant change to slow motion led her leisurely down the hallway to their room. Gregg turned to wave a greeting to their fellow holiday revelers.

Heather was in the bathroom, sick with fear. Gregg satisfied himself that his wound was nothing to worry about, then took out a clean handkerchief and improvised another bandage.

Slowly the door opened and an ashen Heather emerged, holding a damp washcloth to her forehead.

Gregg asked gently, "Are you okay?"

"I'll come about, love. Let's wait a bit."

Now Gregg had a thin steel rod in his hand and was bending the tip with the pliers.

"What is that, Gregg?" Color slowly returned to Heather's cheeks.

"I'm not much good with this thing," he told her, "but we may have to try it." He checked his watch again. "Ready?"

She nodded and followed him out into an empty hallway.

Gregg tried one more time with the steel strip, then brought out the thin rod and worked it into the keyhole, probing, feeling, twisting the thin sliver of steel.

The snap of the lock was so sharp and loud it startled both of them. They stepped inside 221.

Heather took her post by the door, embarrassed at being in a man's room. Quickly Gregg bent over the heater unit and attacked the screws. He set the front cover to one side and started groping underneath. He accidentally touched the heating element and jerked his hand back, scraping it on the sharp frame.

"Turn that thermostat down!"

He knelt to his task again, mumbling to himself, "It must be here. It has to be here."

Gregg's fingers closed upon something soft, and he brought out a clear plastic raincoat folded into its snap-shut pouch, dirty and covered with dust balls and cobwebs.

Still grumbling, he tried again, reaching as far up and back as he could. He changed positions and lay on his back, which allowed him to work his arm all the way underneath the unit as his fingers explored the wall, searching, probing for an opening.

There was a crack in the wallboard! He pushed harder, pressing, forcing the material to give. It moved. Barely, but it moved. Sweating, he strained until he wormed his hand through the narrow opening.

A package! Felt and sounded as if it could be newspaper.

Hearing the rustle of paper, Heather watched as Gregg maneuvered his arm and hand and the parcel out from behind the radiator, dust and debris coming with it.

Suddenly there were footsteps, headed for 221.

Heather froze, her scream held back at the last second, eyes saucer-wide in terror. Gregg got to his feet, brushing himself off, leaving the package on the floor as he shoved his wife into the bathroom and closed the door.

A key rattled in the lock, turned. The door opened and a heavily built man lurched into the room. Face flushed, breath coming in short gasps, he stopped when he saw Gregg.

Thinking quickly, Gregg nearly shouted, "Hey, what are you doing here? Who do you think you are?"

The man was drunk. The sallow face registered shock, then anger, then confusion in quick succession. He swayed unsteadily, still holding the room key.

Gregg pressed his momentary advantage, crowding the intruder so he could not see the clothes and suitcase.

The man found his voice. "You're in my room. What are you doin' in my room?"

Gregg took the man's arm and tried to turn him around toward the hall, but the man refused to be turned. Gregg did succeed in slipping the room key from the big man's hand, but the intruder stood his ground.

At that moment the bathroom door opened and Heather emerged, buttoning her blouse. Her face registered shock as she looked at the stranger and then at her husband.

Confused, the intruder squinted and tried to clear his head, but Gregg was already turning him around and out the door.

"We won't say anything about this," Gregg said. "Why don't you go down to the desk and get a key for your room."

Gregg had one arm over the man's shoulder as he steered him toward the stairs. The big man started to turn back to his room, lurched against the wall, then stumbled down the hall. Quickly Gregg went back to Heather and closed the door.

"You were great. Great. Let's move. Get a towel." She needed no urging. "We've got to get this place put back together before that guy gets down to the desk. You clean up the mess while I put this thing back on."

Already he was holding the cover in position with his shoulder, replacing the screws with both hands.

"Hurry," he kept saying, both to Heather and to himself. Heather worked feverishly, using the towel as a broom to sweep the debris under the heater and then wiping off Gregg's handprints. Gregg checked to see that everything was secure.

"What shall I do with this?" She held the towel.

"Wrap the money in it and let's get out of here. You have our key?"

One quick inspection glance around the room, then Gregg motioned toward the door. They just made it across the hall and into their room when they heard voices in the hallway.

Weak and shaking, Gregg leaned against his door and breathed a prayer of thanks. Heather lay face down on the bed. Next to her lay a hotel towel, soiled and only partly covering the gray parcel underneath.

Tuesday, December 25

A light dust of new snow lay softly over the peaceful
countryside as Gregg turned into the lane. Well back from
the road, a simple white farmhouse nestled between a
magnificent pair of leafless elms.

The lane had been cleared, so Gregg had no trouble
guilding the Volvo past the gaunt row of bare poplars,
boundary markers as well as summer windbreak.

The white frame story and a half looked like a Hallmark
cutout. Instead of clapboards running horizontally, the siding
ran vertically, broken by a wide veranda across the front
and decorated with scrollwork under the eave corners and
roof peak. Smooth white mounds around the porch
identified last summer's shrubbery.

The front door of the house flew open and a laughing
girl, perhaps six or seven years old, blonde hair flying, ran
across the porch and across the yard. Her shoes were full of
snow before she had come halfway.

"Uncle Gregg!"

"Jenny!" He picked her up and wrapped his coat around
her. "Where are your hat and coat? You'll freeze."

"Are you Heather?" Jenny's frank blue eyes appraised
the newcomer. She remembered to offer her hand. "My
name is Jenny."

Inside, Heather found herself nearly suffocated under an

avalanche of kisses and excited chatter. She recognized Gregg's mother, Wilma, at once from the many snapshots Gregg had shown her, the short, dumpy figure and the friendly features as pleasant as she had imagined.

Grandmother Richards, elegant in print dress and ruffled apron, moved efficiently around the kitchen, directing the younger hands of her daughter and daughters-in-law.

Gregg's father, Len, still looked the athlete from his earlier years. Spare, graying at the temples, he presided over the clamor with an even-handed grace.

More people kept coming in, each new arrival touching off an explosion of new faces, rambunctious children, more introductions. By the time the turkey was ready, there were nineteen at the big dining room table and seven children at the smaller table in the parlor. Bev, Gregg's sister, sat at the children's table to manage her two and take care of the others.

One big happy family, thought Heather, though something about Uncle Brian made her uneasy.

Gregg's father took his place at the head of the table. Grandmother Richards sat beside him. Clearing his throat for attention, Len began, "I guess I'm the man of the house this year." A sliver of grief ricocheted around the table as everyone momentarily remembered Grandfather's death the previous January.

Bev, in the next room at the little table, kept trying to shush her eighteen-month-old son, Jamie, who noisily insisted on eating at once. Gregg's father continued, "We'll have our thanks and then we'll begin."

The prayer was mercifully brief, shortened perhaps by the loud complaints from little Jamie, who shut up instantly when his mother corked his mouth with a piece of roll.

Still standing, Mr. Richards held the carving knife, a stack of dinner plates at his elbow. Steaming slices were laid across the diminishing stack of plates, Gregg's mother helping portion out dark meat from the huge drumsticks and thighs. The table became a hubbub of activity as the heaping serving bowls made the rounds.

"Hey, Jeff," Gregg said, "that's a new one for Heather." She was watching Jeff, Gregg's brother, mash his sweet potatoes and anoint them with gravy. She could feel her ears warm at being singled out. "She puts gravy on her French fries, though."

"French fries?" Jeff couldn't believe it. "Gravy on French fries?"

"When she can't get vinegar."

Heather was relieved when the conversation took a new tack.

One of the children in the other room must have knocked over a dish, from the sound of things. Paying no attention to the din, Gregg's Aunt Sara asked Heather, "Do you like our country?"

Had everyone stopped talking? Heather hadn't noticed the clock ticking previously; now it was all she could hear. That, and her pounding heartbeat.

Gregg threw in, "She likes it. She got me, didn't she?"

Still unanswered, Sara's question waited. Heather felt suddenly naked. "I've not seen much of it," she began hesitantly. "I like the big farms. They are like ours."

"What do you think of the border?" That question was not family. Dirk, boyfriend of one of Gregg's cousins, had asked that one.

Smiling, Len Richards broke in, a bit too casually, "How would you like to be hit over the head with a turkey bone?" He brandished the long leg bone from which the meat had been stripped clean.

"The wishbone," someone suggested, "break the wishbone." This met with general approval. Len took out the bow-shaped piece and offered it to his mother, then changed his mind and reached across to Heather.

"I doubt that it's dry enough yet, but let's try anyway. Here, you pull with me. You're our newest family member."

"Wish for a boy," Jeff suggested. Everybody laughed. Heather's earlobes felt warm again. "Wish for more snow." Ski-addict Cousin Lisa said that.

"I'll make a wish," Grandmother Richards interrupted in a voice as strong as steel. She glanced at her son, Brian, and went on. "I wish we had a new government. I wish we had freedom again."

Her audience was open-mouthed and silent. She looked around the table: her sons, her daughter, daughters-in-law, grandchildren, the two strangers with cousins Lisa and Lynn, and Gregg's Canadian wife. Grandmother Richards' voice never wavered. "I am an old woman. Let them do with me whatever they will."

The table talk resumed, but the mood had changed. The wishbone never did get broken, Heather remembered later.

When the women had finished the dishes, Gregg wanted to go to the cemetery. Grandmother Richards wanted to go, too. Jeff and Nancy, his wife, offered to come along.

It had started to snow again. Grandmother Richards rode up front, with Gregg driving, and the others climbed in the back. Every time the Volvo hit a bump Heather cringed inwardly. She forced herself to sit back on the seat and hoped she looked more relaxed than she felt.

Snow shrouded the orderly rows of granite at Rome Cemetery. The narrow lanes between the grave plots were drifted almost even with the smooth surface of the grounds. Gregg found the right place only after two false tries.

He stomped a path through the snow, and he and Jeff helped the old woman to the spot where her husband was buried. Shivering, Grandmother Richards kept looking at the name and dates grooved in the cold granite. Shaking her head, she repeated over and over, "I'm glad you're with the Lord. I'm glad you're not suffering any more."

Gregg could barely make out her words as she explained, "He was so hurt when the change came, so hurt. That's when he had his first attack. He never was well after that."

"Grandmother," Jeff said, trying to shelter her with his coat, "we've done everything we can do. We'd better go."

Sobbing, the old woman broke down completely. "They killed him. They killed him." Finally they led her away from the grave. No one said much of anything on the way back.

Their arrival at the house touched off a near riot. No sooner were they inside than the children began jumping up and down and screaming, "They're back. They're back. Let's open the presents."

The excited clan was waiting in the living room. Grandmother took her place in the rocker by the fire. There was hardly space for one more person in the room. Heather felt their entrance had interrupted a thousand conversations. Everybody seemed to belong.

Donna, another cousin, spoke up. "Let's sing Christmas carols."

"On Citizen's Day?" someone asked sarcastically.

"Yes."

"Let's do. Can we?"

"I have no objection." Acting as host, Len Richards gave his permission. Donna began singing "Away in a Manger" and the others joined in.

Heather could not help but notice that none of the smaller children seemed to know the words except to the first song. Jenny did know most of "Silent Night," but the other children did not even know that one.

Gregg caught his father's eye and threw him a questioning look. Len nodded almost imperceptibly. Clearing his throat for attention, Gregg spoke.

"If no one minds, I'd like to read something before we open our gifts."

Heather stole a glance at Dirk. He acted as if he had not heard and kept staring into the fire.

Gregg took a small Bible from his pocket and found the place. Heather had trouble keeping her mind on the words, perhaps because of their familiarity, perhaps for another reason.

Grandmother Richards rocked slowly in cadence with the reading, her lips moving to the familiar words from Luke. Len Richards sat easily in his chair, outwardly calm though Heather, from her position on the couch, could see the muscle in his jaw twitch.

Jeff's eyes never left his brother's face as Gregg read. Nancy, too, listened with almost the same intensity. The reading over, Gregg bowed his head and prayed briefly. His "Amen" was smothered under the children's "That's all, now let's open the presents."

Jenny presided over the gift exchange. "I can do it. I can read them. Let me do it." Climbing over the maze of legs and bodies crowding the floor, Jenny insisted on personally handing each present to the proper recipient.

When the gifts were all distributed, Sara turned off the room lights, so that the only illumination came from the hearth and the diffused reflection from the pole fixture outside. Big snowflakes swirled across the yard. Gregg sat beside the fire, next to Uncle Brian.

Bob, Donna's husband, asked, "Tell us about your work, Gregg."

"Teaching," Gregg answered. "It's the same as teaching anywhere. Most of the time it's great, but we have our days."

"Where do you teach?"

"Lorne Park Secondary. That's high school here, although we have Grade 13 and you don't."

"It's a good thing I sew," Donna, who was expecting, said to Heather. "Whether this will be a boy or girl, I'll still be able to make a lot of the clothes, at least for a little while."

"I like to sew," Heather said. "I have made many of my own things since I was in my teens. Mind you, Mum helped."

"Do you have the same patterns we do?"

"I think so."

"I know you used to. Before . . ."

"I know," Heather said. "Some of our patterns come from Europe, now. I haven't seen any from the States for some time."

Soon the party began to break up. One of the last to leave was Uncle Brian. Gregg had never felt close to him, and it was awkward for him to stay longer than the others.

Finally able to climb the stairs, Gregg found his father waiting for him in the bathroom. Motioning for Gregg to come in, Mr. Richards closed the door. He talked in whispers.

"What time are you leaving?"

"We'll need to go right after breakfast."

"That's too soon, but we're glad you could come at all."

"I'm glad, too, Dad."

"Did Heather enjoy her day? I like her, Gregg. She's a good girl."

"Thanks, Dad."

"She and Donna seemed to hit it off together."

"I noticed. I wish they could come and see us."

That reminded Len Richards of an unpleasant duty. "By the way," he said, almost apologetically, "I'll have to copy the number off your passport and visa."

"Even though I'm your son?"

Len motioned for Gregg not to talk so loudly. "Even though you're my son, I still have to register you. I need Heather's, too."

"You didn't have to last summer, did you?"

"No, but that was last summer."

"Things are that bad?"

Len Richards raised his hands, then dropped them.

Gregg pressed the issue. "How are you and Mom doing?"

"We're getting along."

"I wasn't sure if I should ask, Dad."

"I know. It's terrible when you can't be free to speak in your own house." He paused, then, "Something went out of your mom when Dad died, but we're all right. Do you remember the Taylors?"

"Paul? Down the road?"

"Yes. The police came into their place last week and went through the house from roof to cellar."

"What for?"

"Who knows?"

"Did they arrest him?"

"No, fortunately. But it's hard not to let that get to you."

"I can imagine. What about your work?"

"There's still pressure, but they've pretty much given up on me. For the most part they leave me alone. I've had my last promotion, of course."

"Dad, is . . . is Uncle Brian, is he . . .?"

Again, Mr. Richards raised his hands and dropped them, a gesture of futility. He looked past Gregg's shoulder as if trying to see through the door into the hallway.

Gregg kept his voice low. "Will you get in trouble over today?"

"I don't think so. What if I do? We weren't having a service, only singing and reading some Scripture."

"You're not allowed to have services?"

The sarcasm came through in spite of the whispering.

"Yes, we're allowed. Providing it's in the approved place, at the approved time, on the approved day, singing the approved songs, with the approved preacher, on the approved subject."

Gregg had difficulty keeping his voice down. "They even give orders what to preach?"

"No, not exactly. The restrictions are that we cannot give an invitation, nothing inflammatory, no politics, as they interpret the word politics. Our preachers have to be very, very careful." He glanced at his watch. "Gregg, we need to be in bed."

"I wish we could talk longer. We really haven't had a chance to talk together all day."

"We're thankful you could even have this one day, and that we could be together at all. Especially with Heather. And at Christmas."

"Especially because it's Christmas," Gregg repeated.

"Citizen's Day," his father said bitterly. He thought of something else. "Gregg, are you still . . .?"

Gregg nodded.

"Where are you going from here? No, don't tell me. Someone may want to know."

Gregg soundlessly pointed in the direction south.

"Gregg, if you're going into West Virginia, be careful. Be extra careful."

"We'll be all right, Dad."

"You're not by yourself this time."

"Dad, it's all right."

"You know there is nothing I can do for you if anything happens."

"I know."

His father wanted to say something more, but Gregg refused to hear it. "We'll be all right, Dad. Don't worry."

"Gregg"—Len looked hard at his son—"I hear things are really bad in West Virginia."

Gregg reached for the doorknob, but his father held his arm. "Do you have a special reason for going down there?"

Gregg ignored the question.

"Gregg, if . . ."

But Gregg was already out the door.

Wednesday morning, December 26

Gregg stopped at Coryville for gas.

"Hi." An open-faced lad about seventeen or eighteen greeted them. Gregg pulled the release latch for the hood and got out, throwing on his coat as he did.

"What's Canada like?"

Gregg hesitated, then answered, "It's about like here."

"You live in Toronto?" The boy evidently had seen the dealer sticker on the tailgate.

"Pretty close. We live in Mississauga, on the west side of Toronto."

Waiting for the tank to fill, Gregg had an idea. "You wouldn't know of a place we could get a donut or something, would you?"

The boy pointed to an old brick building on the next corner. "See that place there? That's the best place around."

"Mom's Place" looked as if it had been standing since the Flood. Above the front windows a design in the brickwork proclaimed MARSHALL'S, overshadowing Mom's hand-lettered shutter hanging out over the street.

A little bell on the back of the front door dinged as Gregg opened it for Heather. Evidently Mom didn't like unexpected guests.

A puffing sergeant-type in a starched apron hurried over

with two glasses of water cupped in one palm and two typewritten menus clutched in the other. She laid out the glasses and the menus on the spotless tabletop and caught her breath.

"Are you 'Mom'?" Gregg asked.

"That's me."

"Nice place you have here," said Gregg. "We'd like a little snack. What's good today?"

"There's some of yesterday's pie left," Mom told him, looking at the glass display case at the end of the counter. Mom looked like her restaurant: weather-beaten and a little too old, but *clean* clean.

A truck driver sat at the counter eating a sandwich. A couple of booths away an elderly gentleman slurped his coffee and rattled a newspaper. Not much trade this time of day.

Mom was still listing the snack possibilities.

". . . coconut cream and apple. Or I have fresh bran muffins. Made 'em this morning."

Gregg could hardly believe it. Before he had moved to Canada he had never eaten a bran muffin; since then he hadn't eaten enough. At that moment he decided he wanted a bran muffin more than anything else in the world.

"We'll have two apiece," he told Mom. "And coffee for me and tea for her."

Still puffing, Mom hurried off to the kitchen.

As Gregg was paying the bill, Heather noticed he was making another one of his diagrams on the back of the paper.

Mom had already slammed the drawer shut and was about to hurry off when she saw what Gregg had drawn. She stopped in her tracks, stared at the paper for a second, and glanced quickly around the room. With a steady hand she drew another line, opposite to the one Gregg had drawn, touching at the front and crossing his about four-fifths of the way toward the rear.

Heather gasped. Mom had made a fish.

Habitually breathless, Mom looked at the young couple in front of her. "I knew there was something about you two I liked." For the first time Heather noticed the crinkles

around the corners of Mom's eyes. "Where you kids
headed?"

"We're on holidays, on vacation."

Pretending to ignore them, the trucker sipped his coffee,
antenna out. The old man paid them no attention,
engrossed in his newspaper.

Mom wasn't satisfied yet. "Going south?"

"Not too far. We have to be back by the second."

"Back to where?"

"We're from Canada."

In one smooth motion the man at the counter slid off his
stool, turned, and gave the travelers the once-over. He laid
two dollars on the counter and left. Mom pocketed the
money, then came back to her guests.

Keeping her voice down, she asked Gregg, "Would you
have any . . . books?"

She could not bring herself to say the word. In a voice so
low it could barely be heard, Gregg said it for her.
"Bibles?"

Motionless, she looked at Gregg for a few seconds, then,
a trifle louder than normal, she told him, "I recommend
that garage you just passed. The one right down the street.
The boy there does good work and can probably fix you
up."

Surely the old man could hear that.

Gregg's response matched Mom's suggestion. He
announced, "We'll try it, and thanks again for the muffins."

At the station once more, Gregg pulled in close to the
service bay and unlatched the hood release. He had the
hood up and was looking at the motor when the boy came
out, surprised to see them back so soon.

"Having trouble?"

Gregg leaned over and reached into the motor as if
looking for a loose connection. "Mom says you can use a
few Bibles," he muttered.

The boy looked past Gregg's shoulder, but the windows
on the big service bay doors were steamed over. He could
not see in, and no one could see out.

"How many do you have, sir?"

"How many can you use? A hundred? Two hundred?"

Instead of answering, the boy closed his eyes. "Thank

God," he prayed. "Thank God." For a moment Gregg
thought the boy would start crying.

Then another car pulled up to the pumps, bringing out a
second attendant. Noticing the man's age and new uniform
jacket, Gregg surmised he must be the boss.

How could they get the Bibles out? How many should
they leave with this high school kid? How long would all
this take? What if they were caught? The voice at his ear
brought him back.

"Bring her in," the boy suggested loudly. "We'll take a
look."

Finished with his customer, the other attendant helped the
boy direct Gregg as he inched the Volvo through the
doorway and almost up to the workbench. When he cut the
motor, Gregg could hear the boy talking to the other man.

"Go down to Mom's and get us a couple of hamburgers.
Don't worry about your sandwich, eat it this afternoon. I
want something hot. Get some fries too. You might ask her
if there's some way she can get us a couple of pieces of pie
in a box."

The boy peeled several bills off the roll in his hand and
gave them to his helper. The helper left.

"He just started," the boy explained, then offered his
hand. "I'm Chris Rogers. I'm helping Dad out since I'm not
in school today. You couldn't have picked a better time to
come."

"What about when he comes back?" Gregg asked,
motioning toward the door.

"Mom will take care of him," the boy laughed. "He
won't be back for an hour. Where are the Bibles? How can
I help?"

Moving rapidly, Gregg raised the tailgate, and unscrewed
the two hold-downs over the spare tire, then lifted the cover
to reveal neat rows of the little black books, carefully fitted
into their custom shelving.

Chris let out a whistle of amazement.

"Where do you want them?" Gregg asked.

"I'll go get a box." Chris disappeared into a side room.
He came back a moment later carrying an empty box which
had once held liters of antifreeze.

A bell signaled there was a car out front.

Chris tossed the box to Gregg and hurried out to the pumps. Heather stationed herself so she could see what was happening outside. "They're not coming in," she told Gregg. Chris had finished and was making change. The car pulled away.

"How's it going?" the boy wanted to know.

Gregg did not take time to answer. He emptied the compartment section by section and stacked the little books tightly into the antifreeze carton.

The bell again. Another car.

Distracted momentarily, Gregg dropped the stack in his left hand. Bibles scattered inside the tire well and behind the spare. Feverishly picking up the ones he could find, Gregg fitted them into the box, then lifted out the spare tire and reached in for the ones which had dropped down behind.

"They're coming in," Heather hissed.

Gregg just had time to cram the last two Bibles into the box, fold the lid flaps down, and set the box on the floor when two big men came into the service area.

"Got a flat?" The first man noticed the spare leaning against the wagon. His greeting was friendly enough.

"Checking things over," Gregg answered him.

Inquisitive, the intruder wanted to see inside the car. "I've never looked at one of these before. Where do they make them? You sure got some room back there. Seat come down?" He stepped over the antifreeze box on the floor.

"The seat folds forward and the back comes down. The front ones recline, too."

"Lots of room."

Gregg moved toward the front of the car, still talking. Anything to divert this meddler! "It has a lot of power, too. Fuel injection. Have you ever seen one of those?"

"No need to show me. Don't trouble yourself." Still looking into the back, the man pointed to the framework in the spare tire well and asked, "What're these for?"

Heather's cheeks drained to a pale white. Her eyes never left Gregg's face. It was a good thing the big man had his back to her.

Gregg answered calmly, "They keep things from falling down behind there."

"What do you put back here?" The man was actually straddling the antifreeze box now.

"Anything," Gregg answered, outwardly unruffled. A bead of sweat trickled down his back and he had to will himself to remain calm. As he came back to the rear of the car, he reached his hand between the anchor for the back seat and the quarter panel. "It keeps things from falling down into the well or up into here."

The other man came out of the washroom. "Come on, John," he said, "let's go."

The questions stopped. John's heavy work shoe kicked against the box as he turned to leave and he almost tripped. He gave the box a sideways kick, called to Gregg, "Nice car you have there," and left. Heather started to breathe again.

Immediately Chris picked up the box and headed for the back room. On impulse, Gregg smashed apart his custom book shelves and threw the pieces into the trash barrel. He was wrestling the spare tire into the compartment when Chris returned.

Chris said nothing as he watched Gregg replace the cover over the tire and rearrange their suitcases and other belongings.

"Time to go, brother," Gregg told him. Heather was already in the car.

"We don't even have time to pray together," Chris said. The bell clanged for another car out front. "But I'll be praying for you."

"Thanks, friend. We need it, and we'll be praying for you."

A few minutes after noon they reached the crossing point. Across the river, Huntington, West Virginia, stretched herself comfortably along the smooth river, accepting the broad river plain as her due, devouring the tableland and expanding beyond the floodwall on out into the hills.

Government policy favored Huntington. West Virginia coal meant energy and power for the Central Region, and Huntington was river port for the inexhaustible mines downstate. There was no urban blight in Huntington.

Cabell-Huntington Hospital was building again. Marshall University was expanding. A new Department of Marxism would take over Central Christian's building, left vacant by their recent merger with Sixth Avenue Church.

Public money supported the downtown renaissance. On the site of Johnson Memorial Methodist's old building now rose a sixteen-story Department of Resources. Fifth Avenue Baptist had become a nursing home. The City Market had long ago been asphalted over for municipal parking. Even the Salvation Army was gone, phased out by Charleston's new Social Benefit Program.

Across the river the two "tourists" knew none of this. Gregg had his mind on something else.

The line moved at irregular intervals. Gregg could detect no pattern, no rhythm. They might sit in the same place for ten minutes, then move forward one car length, or they might wait only a minute or two before moving a car length, or two or three. It took them forty minutes to reach the halfway point on the bridge, from which point they could see the other side.

"Look at that," Gregg grumbled. "No wonder we're taking so long."

Traffic coming off the bridge was divided among four inspection lanes, each complete with separate booth and security personnel. Uniformed guards manned the checkpoint at regular intervals along the chain link boundary fence.

Heather gasped, "It's just like the Peace Bridge."

His response was grim. "You better hope it's not."

Heather twisted in her seat and looked back the way they had come, but there was no room to turn around now.

"Hey"—Gregg tried to soothe her—"we're okay." He put his hand on her arm.

"I'm afraid, Gregg."

"We'll be all right."

Even as he spoke, he kept his eyes on the activity below, trying to put together every scrap of data he could assimilate before their turn came. He noticed that two cars had passed through the second lane in the same time it took for one car in Lane One. *Try to get into the second lane.*

Suddenly conscious of being cold, Gregg realized that Heather had rolled down her window. She had her head back against the door frame, her eyes closed.

"Hey," he said, gently this time, "we'll be all right."

She made no reply.

"Hon," Gregg advised, "better sit up and look natural. Try to."

She pulled herself together, but made no move to close the window opening. Gregg gave her a wink.

At the barrier they had no choice but to go into the right-hand lane. A young woman emerged from the booth, wearing the same green uniform they had seen at the other borders, followed by two men also wearing the same garb. She was all business.

"From Canada?"

The girl accepted the papers and began to thumb through them. Without looking up, she said, "Please open the back." It was not quite a question.

Gregg got out and raised the rear door. Still holding the documents, the girl approached him. "What do you want?"

Gregg did not understand what she meant. "Do you mean a 'transit visa' or what?"

The inspector's brows furrowed. She looked at Gregg as if he were illiterate. "What I mean is, how long do you intend to stay?"

Why was he letting her make him nervous?

Silently the two men stood by the car, unfeeling, staring. Gregg had to make himself speak. "We'd like to stay two days."

"Where do you want to go?"

Maddening, these questions. Gregg reached for some kind of an answer. Under other conditions he would have thought this girl attractive. Not now.

"My wife likes to paint," he answered. "We hope to sketch some mountains."

With a quick nod to the two men, the girl turned on her heel and went inside the booth. In two minutes the pair had sifted through the assortment of boots, coats, suitcase, overnighter, and Gregg's box of extra oil. Gregg had to open the suitcase, but the older officer hardly looked inside.

The younger guard was more diligent. He pointed to the compartment on the right side. "What's in there?"

"The window washer bottle," answered Gregg, lifting off the compartment lid. The guard looked in at the reservoir and pump and ran his hand between the rear wheel arch and the quarter panel.

The center compartment was next. This took only a few moments. Then he tapped the left side. "What's in there?"

"The spare tire."

As directed, Gregg unscrewed the cover piece and lifted it off to expose the spare. Gregg started to lift out the tire, but the guard stopped him and walked around to the far side of the car. Gregg opened the back door, but the guard barely looked inside. Moving to the front seat, he motioned for Heather to get out.

She swung her feet around and took a couple of steps away from the car. The guard sat down half in and half out of the car and began rummaging through the glove box.

Down here the air seemed warmer, Gregg thought. The inspection plaza had once been a four-lane street. The surrounding buildings blunted the force of the wind. The row of billboards lining the top of the buildings probably helped too, though their propaganda slogans did nothing for Heather.

For the most part the area was clean. Yesterday's snow was plowed to one side in a huge gray wall.

Heather watched the guard, now on his hands and knees, feeling underneath the front seat and the seat cushion.

The guard motioned for Gregg to close the tailgate, and he and his companion moved off. Gregg accepted their papers from the woman, and he and Heather were on their way. The clock read 1547.

Two minutes later and 520 kilometers to the east, a black limousine came to a stop outside the main entrance to the Department of Security, six blocks from the White House. Quickly a uniformed attendant emerged, saluted smartly, then opened the door for the fat man in the back seat. Head throbbing from too much holiday leave, Bert Wilson, Director for Internal Security, was finally coming back to his office. That morning's four hours of conferences and a working lunch had done little for his stomach and nothing for his disposition. This afternoon he intended to attack the inevitable pile of reports which would have accumulated on his desk during the two days' absence.

Wednesday afternoon, December 26

Except for the ever present police, downtown Huntington showed little sign of hardship under the new regime. Most of Fifth Avenue was either new or being rebuilt. Construction crews toiled away, ignoring the bitter weather.

The heavy traffic slowed Gregg to a crawl, and when he saw a car pulling out from the curb he quickly put the Volvo into the parking space.

"Let's see"—he looked around—"we're across from the library."

"Fifth Avenue and Ninth Street," Heather added.

"Let's find a good place to eat."

"I don't think it's as cold as it has been." (She pronounced "been" to rhyme with "seen.")

Gregg would have walked right past John's Cafeteria, but Heather caught his arm. It was so crowded Gregg had trouble finding a table to themselves.

"Good roast beef," he said after they had finally sat down.

"Mine, too."

"People look pretty well off, don't they?" he observed.

"At least those in here."

"Maybe the have-nots can't even afford this."

"Are there things to see here?" Heather asked.

"Tonight we'll see the Lamberts," Gregg said, knowing that wasn't what she meant. He read the fear on her face and changed the subject.

Outside the temperature had dropped a point or two, but the day was not uncomfortable.

"I don't know about you," Gregg said to his wife, "but I need to walk off some of that."

"Yes," she said, "I would enjoy that."

A series of small shops lined Ninth Street. Heather enjoyed comparing prices and quality with what she was used to in Toronto. They turned a corner and started up Fourth Avenue.

A uniformed officer stood in the middle of the sidewalk, confronting a middle-aged couple and questioning them. The man had his billfold out and was showing his papers to the policeman.

"No, you don't," Gregg said under his breath as Heather started to turn around. "Come on."

"Gregg . . ."

"We're going right on by," he told her. "Just act natural."

Gregg nudged her toward a department store. By going in one entrance and sauntering casually through the store and leaving by the far entrance Gregg was able to steer around the policeman.

"What was he doing?" Heather inquired as soon as it was safe to ask.

"Checking their papers."

"Right on the street?"

"You saw it as well as I did."

"Gregg, I cannot believe it. Stopping their own people on the street."

"One of the blessings of their system," Gregg said sarcastically.

Gregg turned right at Tenth Street, taking a quick look backward to determine the whereabouts of the officer.

"Is he coming?" Heather asked.

"No. He's still back there. He has someone else cornered."

Heather shuddered. She had lost all interest in the display windows.

Seeing a phone booth, Gregg walked over to it, but came back in disgust.

"No book," he explained.

"What were you looking for?"

"A city map."

"Don't you know where their place is?" She talked as if

she were afraid the other shoppers would overhear and find out what they were discussing.

"I know the address, but I don't know where the street is. It's Norway Avenue, wherever that is."

"We could drive and we might find it."

"We could try, but I want to be able to drive straight there."

"And not be noticed."

"Right. If I only had a . . . ." He stopped in mid-sentence. Heather saw them, too. Two foot patrolmen halfway down the block, coming this way.

"Here," Gregg suggested, "in the drugstore."

Inside, Heather followed her husband as he slowly made the rounds between the shelves. He picked up a bottle of aspirin and a couple of postcards.

Heather noticed the lack of competing brands. There were rows of toothpaste, but all the same brand. Only one brand of bath soap, too. The same with shampoo, with hair creme, with everything.

In spite of the ample supply of approved brands, many places on the shelves were simply devoid of anything. Display signs and posters partially covered the open spaces.

"Do you have stamps?" Gregg asked the girl at the cash register.

"No, we don't. You'll have to get them at the post office."

"No problem. Thanks anyway. What time does the post office close?"

"Five o'clock, today," the girl said. "You're not from around here, are you?"

"We're on holidays," Gregg answered as he and Heather made for the door. The two policemen were nowhere in sight.

Sitting in the car, Gregg took out the postcards and gave one to Heather. "Let's send one to your folks, to let them know we're okay. I'm going to let Dad know we made it across with no problems."

"What will I say?"

"Say whatever you want to, so long as you don't care

who reads it. Say you're having a good trip and that we'll be home on Monday."

For a few minutes both of them were silent, busy writing. Gregg left Heather in the car while he walked across the street to the post office.

When he returned he told her, "I saw another policeman stopping people and inspecting their papers."

"Love, may we drive around? I don't like sitting here."

"Do you suppose this is a regular thing? They might be looking for someone," Gregg commented without thinking.

Heather grabbed his arm and almost screamed, "Gregg, could they be looking for us?"

"No, hon,"—he tried to calm her—"they're not looking for us."

Bert Wilson grunted as he slowly worked his way down through the mountain of papers. He picked up one of Callihan's Daily Reports, from the Midwest District. Wilson skimmed over the sheet and started to lay it aside when he caught the data on the white Volvo from Canada. He read the words slowly again, each word making him draw his brows closer together as he gnawed on his cigar.

Rumbling like a volcano about to explode, Wilson muttered to himself, "Who does he think is running this operation? *He* decides to call off *my* order?"

A fat forefinger stabbed the intercom. "Get Bill Simpson in here."

"Yes, sir."

"And call Columbus and put Larry Callihan on the phone. If he's not in his office, tell them to find him and have him call me back—right away."

Moments later a lanky figure stood before Wilson. Simpson's eyes darted this way and that as he listened to his boss's instructions.

"Friday this Volvo entered from Canada. Here's the number and description. Here is where they've been, up to Monday afternoon. Find out where they went after that and what they're doing now. No arrests. Not yet. I want to know who these people are and what they're doing down here."

"Do you have any leads to go on?"

"No. That's for you to develop. Check state line crossings, motels, traffic reports. Go the whole route. You might have to wait until we have tonight's list of registrations. I'll get you clearance on the computer if you need it. I want these people found."

Gregg and Heather were enjoying a delightful oasis in the Huntington desert: the Huntington Galleries. A winding road had led them to a modern building high on a hill behind the city. For two hours they meandered slowly past a superb collection of sketches, paintings, pottery, and tapestries. Heather found herself enjoying even the garish examples of socialist realism.

Here no one asked any questions, nor did arrogant inquisitors demand to see citizens' papers. With the approach of darkness, Gregg returned to the business at hand—finding Norway Avenue.

He stopped at a Seven-Eleven, leaving Heather in the car while he went inside. When Gregg came out he was carrying a small grocery bag, but Heather could tell by the look on his face that he still didn't have what he wanted.

"They didn't know where it was," Gregg told her as he started the car, "and when I asked for a city map the woman looked at me as if I were crazy."

"They don't have maps?"

"If her reaction was any clue, there's not a map in this whole place."

Gregg drove back to the downtown area. They were again moving with the eastbound traffic on Fifth Avenue.

"What happened to the people we want to see?" asked Heather.

"He was a preacher. When the change came, he didn't want to go along with the new restrictions. Classes for children, no invitations—that kind of thing."

"And they put him in jail?"

"They fined him at first. You know—first time a warning, second time a fine, third time a bigger fine."

"And if you continue, then it's prison."

"Right."

They passed a chemical factory on their right, well lit in the darkness. At each entrance a sullen guard sat watching traffic from his illuminated guardhouse, reminding Heather of photographs she had seen of Auschwitz or Dachau.

They read the street signs along Fifth Avenue. None turned out to be Norway. As Gregg crossed Twenty-ninth, he had another idea.

"Let's see if it's back this way. Maybe they start using names of countries."

Emmons, Guyan, Chesterfield, Latulle, but no Norway. Just then they passed a dilapidated filling station. "That guy can help us; I'll bet on it," Gregg said optimistically. Pulling up to the pumps, he wondered why an old man would still be working on a winter evening.

"Fill it up," Gregg said. "Say, you wouldn't happen to have a city map?"

Keeping his eyes on the moving numbers the old man answered, "Behind the door."

The station looked as if it ought to retire. Gregg found the map, faded and dirty, but there was Norway. He pinpointed their location and memorized the layout of the streets he would have to take.

"We were real close," he told Heather as soon as they were moving again. "Back at Twentieth Street we should have turned."

"Gregg," she began, "could we pray?"

He had been thinking the same thing. There were no street lights along here, so Gregg stopped the car and turned off the lights.

He reached for Heather's hand. "Let's pray that we'll meet Mrs. Lambert if it's the Lord's will, and that we can give her the money without causing her any trouble."

"Or causing any for us."

"Or any for us," he repeated.

Heather's apprehension mounted as they wound around the hill going out Norway and swept past a gloomy cluster of buildings on the left. A hospital or a prison—it was hard to tell in this blackness.

"We have to be close," Gregg told her.

All at once he stiffened. Before she could ask what was

wrong, Heather's ears picked up the faint wail of a siren, quickly becoming louder. Turning around, she could see flashing red lights rapidly overtaking them.

"It can't be," Gregg said under his breath.

The rise and fall increased to a shriek as the hunter closed for the kill. Gregg braked and pulled over to the curb. The lights and blare swept past.

It was an ambulance.

Someone else was in trouble tonight. Not them. Not yet. Gregg let out a nervous laugh. "There went ten years of my life."

"Mine, too." Heather could hardly talk, she was shaking so much.

Gregg made a left, then a right, parking on East Oakland.

"How many Bibles will we give away this time?" Heather asked.

"None this time."

She didn't understand.

"If we happen to be seen," Gregg explained, "I don't want to be carrying anything."

"Seen by whom?"

Gregg didn't answer.

"Love," she asked him, "is their house being watched?"

Still Gregg didn't answer. Heather was suddenly very, very cold in spite of her heavy wrap. Silently she followed Gregg as they walked back out to Norway, then down the long hill.

The sidewalk was on the left side, and every oncoming car pinned them momentarily in its headlight beams. Heather flinched each time and tucked her chin down inside her collar.

"How much farther, love?"

"It can't be far. Should be in the next block, if these numbers are right. Maybe it's that big apartment building."

Gregg's guess proved correct. They entered the dark hallway, momentarily glad for the warmth. Gregg fumbled through his pockets, failed to find what he was looking for, went through his pockets again, muttering in self-reproach.

"Of all the stupid things."

"What's the matter?" Heather whispered.

"I forgot the flashlight."

"Oh."

Gregg went through his pockets again. Comb. Keys. Billfold. Penknife. Pen. Change. No flashlight.

He whispered, "Do you have any matches?"

"No. Sorry."

The hallway was almost totally dark. A set of stairs rose against the far end of the hall, and the glassed in area behind the stairs provided a faint light, so Gregg could make out the shape of objects in one direction, but could see nothing in the other.

He groped for Heather's hand.

"Come on," he whispered, "let's try upstairs."

Cautiously Gregg led the way to the stairs. In the darkness he stumbled on the second step and nearly dragged Heather down with him as he fell, her startled scream stifled in her throat.

For several seconds Gregg sat motionless, listening to see whether the clatter had sounded an alarm. In the black silence he could hear Heather's quick breathing, but nothing else.

The second floor was as dark as the first. Gregg felt his way along the wall to a door. His fingertips located a knob and continued to survey the flat smooth surface until they touched something else. A small rectangular frame, a holder, with a card in it. This might be what he was looking for. If he could only see it.

He put both hands flat against the door and brought his face up to the card, straining to focus his eyes. He was able to make out the shape of the frame and the faint whiteness of the card, but not the writing. Gregg tried the other doors with no better results. Without a flashlight or a match, he might as well have been blind.

Heather gasped as he touched her, to lead her toward the stairs again and the third floor. He had to either find the right apartment or get out of there. He knew Heather couldn't take much more.

They had just reached the third floor landing when a door opened above them and they heard voices. Instantly Gregg reversed courses and, still clutching Heather's hand, dragged her back down the stairs.

Suddenly the whole scene was flooded with dazzling brightness. The person upstairs had flipped on the hall lights.

Not two feet in front of him Gregg saw a doorway, one of those he had tried earlier. The card read PASTOR WILLIAM LAMBERT. *Thank you, Lord.* Quickly he tapped the door twice.

It was opened by a blonde woman not quite thirty, wearing a robe and slippers. Wordlessly she motioned for them to come inside. Upstairs, footsteps sounded across the floor to the stairs. Gregg closed the door, leaving the hallway empty for whoever was approaching.

Gregg kept his voice low. "I'm Gregg Richards. This is my wife, Heather."

"I'm Janice Lambert. You are welcome here."

Their hostess led them through the dark living room into a dining nook between the front room and the kitchen. Three glasses of milk, two of them half empty, were set out on the table. Mrs. Lambert closed the door between them and the kitchen, isolating their tiny cubicle.

Gregg squeezed into a chair between the table and the wall, Heather sitting across from him. Janice took the end chair. Behind her a manger scene was arranged on the sideboard.

"I hope we didn't startle you too much by coming unannounced like this."

"Please don't apologize. When I saw you, I knew you must be believers."

"We certainly don't want to create any problems for you."

"You won't. I am glad you're here."

A door creaked behind Heather, startling her. Gregg and Janice laughed as a little girl, barefoot and dressed in nightclothes, peered around the doorway.

"Look who's here," Janice said, her tired face smiling a welcome to the child. She held out her hand, and the little girl ran into her arms and crawled up into her mother's lap.

Janice spoke into the darkness of the bedroom. "You may come out, too." Out came a boy, six, and a girl, eight, the older girl a miniature of her mother.

Apologetically, Janice explained, "When we heard your

knock, we weren't sure who it might be, so the children went to their room."

Was it imagination, or did Heather really see a wave of apprehension cross the little girl's face at this reminder?

"Tell us about yourself," Janice asked. "Where are you from?"

"We're from Toronto, Canada."

"And you came all that way to see us?" There, again. That flicker of fear. Only this time on the mother.

Gregg noticed it, too. "We had another reason for coming." He looked at Heather. "You see, I'm an American. My folks had never met Heather. I wanted them to meet her."

Janice looked relieved. "I didn't introduce you to the children. This is Karen, Andrew, and Lynn."

"Do you know my Daddy's in jail?" eight-year-old Karen asked Heather.

"Yes, dear," Heather answered, "we know, and we're sorry."

"He's at Moundsville," Andy put in. "We write letters to him."

"And he writes back to you?" Heather asked hesitantly.

"Sometimes."

His mother added, "Bill is permitted to write one letter a week."

"Tell me about your school," Heather suggested to Karen. "What grade are you in?"

Karen showed little enthusiasm. "The third."

"Do you like school?"

Karen looked at her mother, unsure how much to tell this stranger. "I like part of school and I don't like part of school."

"What about school do you like most?" Heather asked.

Andy put in, "Recess."

"Christmas vacation," Karen said.

"Don't say 'Christmas,' " corrected Andy.

"We still say 'Christmas,' don't we?" Heather said gently.

"Yeah," echoed Andy.

Heather couldn't resist a glance toward the living room. As if reading the unspoken thought, Janice answered, "We didn't have a tree. The children and I set up the manger scene." Looking at her brood, she continued, "We had presents, too, didn't we?"

"Yeah," they agreed.

Karen added, "Even for Daddy."

Janice explained, "I can visit Bill once a month and can bring him a few things."

"The children don't go with you?"

"They stay here. One of the girls in the church stays with them while I'm gone."

"How is the church doing?" Gregg asked.

"Well enough." The look on Jan's face betrayed her noncommittal answer. "How is the church in Canada?"

Gregg sensed Heather's sympathy with this young mother left alone at Christmas, struggling to keep going. He chose his words carefully as he answered Jan's question.

"Our churches are doing well. Some are large, but most are small. Conditions down here have been hard for you, I know, but I think what has happened here has made our churches stronger."

Jan's face remained impassive as she half-listened to Gregg.

"Across the board," he continued, "I would say that our churches are more serious and determined than they ever have been."

Jan's expression showed that she understood. Gregg tried another tack, hopefully less painful.

"Heather and I go to church in a shopping mall. Property is so high in our area that this seemed to be the best solution."

"Is this a regular church?"

Gregg let Heather answer. "Yes. We rent enough space for our worship services and for classes for the adults and children."

Jan looked at her little ones. "Neither of my babies has been in Bible school. Do you have to register?"

"Not as you do here. All the government wants to know is whether we are a legitimate nonprofit organization."

To Jan, that seemed a marvel beyond words. "It used to be that way here, such a long, long time ago."

Lynn had gone to sleep on her mother's lap. "I think," Jan said to the two children still awake, "it's time for my sleepyheads to be in bed."

"We need to go." Gregg started to work his way out of his cramped position between the table and the wall, but Jan stopped him.

"Please don't. I'll only be a minute and then we can have a cup of tea together. I'm sorry I don't have any coffee."

With the children in bed, Jan opened up more to her guests. "There are times when I don't think I can hold on. I thought it was difficult at first, but it seems to become worse instead of better."

Gregg let Jan talk.

"It's so hard on the children. They're so young. I've tried to explain, but it's hard for them to understand."

"Yes, it would be."

"The hardest is when the other kids make fun of them." Now Jan was sobbing. "They say such harsh things. The first day of school, Karen came home early, crying. She didn't want to go back the second day, but I walked with her and made her go. She keeps saying, 'Daddy's not a bad man, Mommy. Why is he in jail?' "

"Are the church people helping you?"

A confused expression developed on Jan's face and was quickly banished. Her words came slowly. "Some have. Some have been wonderful to us. We've had our disappointments, too."

Gregg said it for her. "When you're in trouble, you find out who your friends are."

"You surely do." Jan hastened to add, "I don't want to complain though. The Lord is helping us through this thing."

Heather spoke now. "He's there when we need Him, isn't He?"

"He is always there," Jan agreed. "Without Him, I don't know what we would have done."

"I've seen it before," Gregg said. "The worst thing about the system is the way it divides people from each other." Jan nodded in agreement as Gregg went on, "It separates people, even Christian people if we're not careful."

Gregg half rose out of his chair and worked a thick envelope out of his pants pocket. He had put the money in one of the envelopes from The Stone Lodge.

Laying the parcel on the table in front of Jan, he explained, "This is a gift from your brothers and sisters who want you to know that we are with you and are praying for you."

Jan was sobbing audibly now, then quieted down so the children wouldn't hear her. She spoke with difficulty. "How can I tell you what this means to us?"

"Open it," Gregg urged.

Jan gasped when she saw the stack of twenty dollar bills. "That's D.R.A. money, Jan, as you can see, and it's all twenties. You won't have to explain to anyone where it came from."

Jan wiped her eyes, still crying. "It's so much."

"We only wish it were more," Gregg said.

The three of them went into the living room as Jan talked. "The church at Charleston lost their building. They were told the building was needed for a nursery school, so since September they have been meeting in homes."

"Are they meeting without registration?"

"Yes. The officials won't let them register. I just wanted you to know, so you could pray."

"Is there something we can do?"

"I don't know. I don't even know where they are meeting or how to tell you to get in touch with anyone."

"Do you have any addresses? Anything?"

"No. Nothing at all."

For a moment no one spoke. Gregg finally said, "Let's pray together, and then we must go." Heads bowed, hands joined, the three formed a triangle in the darkness of the front room, their silhouettes outlined on the hallway door and wall.

Shortly before midnight Bill Simpson put together the last piece of data for his report to Wilson. He knew his boss was working late and wanted to see this report before he went home.

Summoning his courage, Simpson walked down the empty

hallway, past the desk where Wilson's secretary guarded the inner sanctum during the day, and tapped on the door.

"I found them." Simpson told his boss, as triumphantly as his thin voice would allow.

Wilson grunted approval. "Let me see what you have."

He read aloud as he scanned the paper. "Mountain State Motel. St. Albans. Mr. and Mrs. G. Richards. Why these Canadians don't use their full names is beyond me. Registered one night. What is he doing in West Virginia?"

Looking up at his clerk, Wilson asked, "What time did this come in?"

"It just came over on the last report." Simpson checked his watch. "It must have been about 11:00 or 11:15."

Wilson returned to the paper. "Not hard to follow them, at least. This must be his father. The others must be relatives. No problems crossing out of Ohio."

Wilson shifted his cigar to the other corner of his mouth, took a deep drag, and blew a cloud of smoke toward the ceiling. For several seconds he stared at his clerk, who grew more uncomfortable under the glare from those eyes.

What Simpson failed to realize was that his boss didn't even see him. To Wilson he was an object, a thing, part of the furniture. Simpson stood up straighter as his boss dictated his orders.

"I've got a feeling about this character. We'll keep an eye on those two. Tell Charleston to put a tail on them. I want to know where he goes, everyone he sees, everything he does. Tell them to crowd this Richards."

"Yes, sir."

"Take care of that before you leave."

"Yes, sir."

"I want a car on them when they pull out of that motel."

Thursday, daylight, December 27

"See anything you want to sketch?" Gregg asked as they came into Charleston proper.

"Not really."

Threading his way through the morning traffic, Gregg turned onto a boulevard running alongside the Kanawha. The sluggish river flashed iridescent blues and reddish greens back at them.

"I'll bet this is beautiful in the summer."

Gregg picked out a distinctive shape ahead. There, he could see it again. "We'll find you something yet," he told his wife.

Now Heather could see it, the graceful dome of the capitol rising above the trees. As they drove to it, sunlight glinted on the gilded mass towering over the limestone and marble corridors. The front vestibule looked like a miniature Parthenon with its stone symmetry.

"Oh, it's lovely. Can we stay here for a bit?"

"Sure."

Gregg carried the camera, while Heather brought her sketchbook and a couple of charcoal pencils. He used his camera as an excuse to survey the area, but didn't see anyone who seemed to be interested in them. Heather, sitting on one of the steps, made preliminary sketches she could complete later. Two men, properly fitted out with attaché cases and all-weather topcoats, came out of the building, but neither gave Gregg a second look.

He climbed the front steps and started to saunter inside. A surly guard immediately blocked his way.

"Do you have a pass?"

Startled, Gregg blurted, "No, sir. I was just looking around." Spotting the massive chandelier hanging in the rotunda, Gregg asked if he could take a picture.

The guard hesitated. "Unless you have a pass you are not permitted inside."

"I don't need a flash," Gregg told the guard. "I could take it from right here."

Scowling with impatience, the guard capitulated. "Step in a little ways. It may as well be a good one."

Gregg cocked the timer, opened the lens all the way, and held his elbows against his body as he aimed the camera upward. He didn't breathe until he heard the click as the shutter snapped.

With a quick thank you to the guard he stepped back outside into the sunshine. He felt slightly like an inmate walking into freedom after a prison sentence.

Heather was finishing her drawing. A young couple passed them, hatless, ski tags pinned to their jackets, the girl's blonde mane streaming in the wind.

Gregg moved around behind his wife and watched. She added a stroke, looked up at the dome, looked away, returned again to the drawing. A touch here, another line there. With a minimum of bold, sure strokes she had captured the mass and grace of the front portico. Fainter lines suggested the wings on either side.

Gregg was as amazed by what she had omitted as much as by what she had included. Even to his untrained eye there were gaps in the curved outline of the dome and the rectangular wings. She had left out whole sections, offering a quick slash or merely a shadow to convey a window or cornice. But the effect was breathtaking in its simple clarity.

The noon rush had cleared out by the time they were ready to eat. Gregg left Heather in the car while he went inside a fast food place for some hamburgers. He came out carrying two sacks and a disappointed look.

"Is something the matter?" Heather asked.

"No." Gregg tried to play down his feelings.

"Love, what's wrong?"

"I just asked the girl if she knew of any church around here, and she said there wasn't any."

"Is that all?"

He didn't answer, but opened their bags and set out their lunch.

An older couple drove up and as the man and woman got out of their car, Gregg rolled down his window.

"I wonder if you could help us," he asked the woman. Warily, she edged away. "Do you know if there's any church in the area?"

The woman acted as if she had not heard, then glanced at her husband who ever so lightly shook his head. Gregg knew the man had heard the question, but repeated it anyway. "Can you help us?"

The man made no answer, but took his wife's elbow and steered her toward the restaurant and safety. Stunned, Gregg looked at Heather. "What about that? If they knew, they sure weren't telling."

"Love,"—there was a note of fear in her voice—"let's not stay here."

"We'll try a gas station," Gregg said, heading toward the boulevard again.

They came to a large franchise station, but Gregg drove on past. Several blocks farther was a small two-pump affair. Gregg tried that.

"Warmed up, hasn't it?" he asked the operator, who seemed to be by himself.

"Yep. Won't be as cold tonight."

"What's the forecast?"

"Don't know. Ain't had the radio on."

"Think it will snow?"

"Might. Soon's the sun goes down it's cold enough. Might rain if it don't snow."

Gregg made his move. "You don't know of any church around here, do you?"

The man flinched and released his hold on the nozzle, stopping the flow of gasoline. "Young fellah, don't be asking questions like that."

He stepped back and looked at Gregg's rear license plate,

then started pumping gas again. "You're not from around here, so let me offer you a suggestion. Don't make trouble for yourself."

"What do you mean?"

"Just what I said. Don't make trouble for yourself."

Gregg handed the man money for the gas and tried again as the attendant counted out change.

"I'm not asking for trouble," Gregg told the man. "We just want to find a church."

The man turned away. Gregg tried to follow him inside, but the attendant waved him on.

"You'd think I wanted to commit murder," Gregg complained to Heather.

"Love," she began, "can't we give up this time?"

He gently cut her off. "We'll give it one more try, okay? How could we . . . a cab driver would know!"

They drove on for several blocks. Heather thought what she saw was a church, but it turned out to be a moving company. The structure had originally been built for a church, but that was long ago.

They both saw a taxi at the same time, coming right toward them. Despite Gregg's frantic attempts to catch the driver's attention, he went on by. Gregg turned around, trying to keep the cab in sight. He worked his way through the traffic, but the cab was too far ahead to overtake.

Suddenly the cab pulled over to the curb, but Gregg's elation was short-lived. The taxi had stopped behind a police car, and the driver was talking with one of the patrolmen as the Volvo drove past.

"Here we are—a load of Bibles and nobody to give them to."

Now he felt ashamed. "Tell you what," he said to Heather. "From this point we do nothing. We'll give it to the Lord. If He wants us to make contact tonight, then we let Him lead the way."

Heather listened but didn't comment.

Gregg talked as he drove south toward the city limits. "We'll get out of town and just drive. We'll trust God to lead us to the people who need these Bibles and ask Him to help us find a way to deliver them."

At the east end of Charleston Gregg had to choose

between the West Virginia Turnpike or Route 60. He decided against the toll road with its exit gates and fenced in roads.

Route 60 snaked along the river, the hills cutting off the sunshine as the road wound through the valley. Heather reached for the heater knob. To her this was an unfriendly world, jerry-built shanties huddled against the hillsides, black rock showing through the thin snow cover as dark stains.

"How do these people make their money?" she asked.

As if in answer a huge coal truck rounded a curve. "Probably work in Charleston," Gregg suggested, "or in the coal mines. I guess . . ." Gregg stopped in mid-sentence when he noticed that traffic had come to a standstill. *What now?* he wondered.

"Those are company houses, I'll bet," he told Heather. She had her sketchbook out, quickly putting down impressions of the drab row of copper-colored shells.

"Must be a wreck up ahead," Gregg said.

Heather was so busy drawing that Gregg saw the roadblock first. A patrol car straddled the center of the highway, forcing traffic from both ways to slow down. A second car was parked slightly ahead of the first and to the right, so that the two cars formed a sort of inspection booth for southbound traffic.

Gregg noted with relief that each car only stopped for a moment, while the officers spoke to the drivers and looked inside before passing the cars through.

"Do you suppose it's us, Gregg?"

"No." He tried to sound convincing. "Maybe someone stole a car or something. They're not looking for us."

Looking over at her, he suggested grimly, "Why don't you draw that?"

She didn't think it was funny.

Their turn finally came. The officer doing the questioning had the look of a man who spends a lot of time outdoors. Another uniformed figure stood behind him, while still another officer, holding a short-barreled automatic rifle, stood next to the right-hand patrol car. A fourth officer directed traffic, keeping the northbound lane moving.

"You're from out of state?"

Obviously, Gregg thought. "Yes, sir," he said.

"Canada?"

"Yes, sir."

"What are you doing this far away from home?"

"I came down, I mean, we came down so my wife could meet my family. We came down for the holidays."

"Your family lives here?"

"Yes, sir."

"In West Virginia?"

"No, sir," Gregg answered reluctantly.

"Your passports and visas, please."

Gregg handed the documents to the officer. He opened Gregg's passport, studied the photograph, and thumbed through the pages, noting each stamp from the places he had registered. He did the same with Heather's, oblivious to the traffic backing up behind the Volvo.

"Do you have any relatives in West Virginia?"

"No."

"Then what are you doing down here burning up our gasoline and using our highways and nosing around our people?"

Heather felt the strongest urge to scream. Gregg tried to answer the man's question. "We're on holidays. My wife paints. Look, here's what she's been doing."

The officer took the sketchbook and leafed through Heather's all too accurate reproductions of the grimy shacks they had just passed. Flaring in anger, he ripped out the drawings, crumpled them into a wad, and threw it at Heather.

"Take that back to Canada with you," he shouted at her, his head in Gregg's window. He handed back the papers and told Gregg to move on.

Shaking, Gregg pulled the selector into gear and drove past the second patrol car. The gun-wielding guard's cold stare transfixed the two travelers passing within an arm's length of his gun muzzle. Heather was crying.

When she could speak, she pleaded, "Gregg, can't we go back into the city now?"

He tried to get himself under control. "Hon, if we go back, we'll have to go right by that roadblock and right past those same guards. Let's go on a little ways."

Still sobbing, Heather asked, "Do you think we'll be able to get out of here?"

He reached across and took her hand. "Hang on, baby. We're still in one piece, and we're together. The Lord's brought us all this way. He's not going to let us down now." *Lord, give me wisdom.*

Gregg turned on the radio.

Alarmed, Heather protested, "You're not going to call Ian?"

"No." He tuned across the dial. Heather started crying harder. "What's wrong, hon?"

"Gregg, please turn it off. It makes me want to go home."

The road forked, and so did the river. Almost at once the whole scene changed. The river made a wide sweep to the right, while to their left a smaller tributary meandered through a picturesque little town on its way to the main stream.

An old railroad bridge linked the two halves of the village. Farther upstream was a smaller one for cars. Above and behind the bridges tier after tier of houses rose nearly all the way up the mountain. Heather was feeling a bit better now.

"Looks like Switzerland," Gregg commented. The road changed and they began climbing, sharp curves and switchbacks taking them higher and higher.

With each turn the view became more spectacular. A sign read HAWK'S NEST PEOPLE'S PARK 15 KILOMETERS. Near the top they passed an overlook, but Gregg wanted to keep going. "The sign says there's an aerial tramway up here. Want to ride it?"

"If you do."

Gregg changed his mind at the park, however. The lodge was lovely enough, set back on the bluff overlooking the river. The tramway was probably on the other side of the building, but the guards at the entrance gates changed his mind. He decided to go back to the overlook.

Heather wanted to stay in the car, but Gregg insisted she get out. Tentatively moving up to the brim, she looked down at a sight which took her breath. She felt as if she were looking down upon creation; only her Eden was a canyon mantled in white, decorated by the frothing stream far, far below.

"It is pretty, isn't it, love," she admitted, holding on to him.

"Want to draw it?"

"I could."

"You stay here," he said, "and I'll get your things. I want to take a couple of pictures, too."

He had not been out two minutes, and already he was cold. As he was getting the camera out of the car, he saw a purple van drive past, slow down, then turn around and come back. Heather gave up on her drawing almost at once, her fingers stiff with the cold.

"I didn't think it got this cold so far south," Gregg complained, shivering, once they were driving again. He had the heater on full. Heather had her boots off and was hunched up to the dashboard, her hands over the defrost outlets and her stockinged feet under the hot blast to the floor.

Odd, how quickly darkness came in these mountains. The heavy clouds moving in had cut off the last of the sun. Gregg switched on the headlights.

"Are we still going to try and contact someone?" Heather asked hesitantly.

"I thought we decided to let the Lord lead."

"But what about the police?"

"What about them? They don't know about us."

"But they do." It started to rain.

"Not about the Bibles." He turned on the windshield wipers.

They came to the place where the roadblock had been set up earlier. Now there was no sign of patrol cars or policemen.

"See," Gregg told her. "No problem."

"Gregg, I'm still afraid."

He tried to reassure her again. "We'll be okay." Then, "I love you."

Her voice was nearly inaudible. "I love you too."

Lights from oncoming cars reflected off the road surface. Gregg felt the rear end slip as he accelerated out of a turn.

"Freezing rain," he explained. "The defroster makes it look like rain, but it's freezing on the road." He used this excuse to flip on the rear defroster and wiper to clear the glass in the tailgate.

Heather had her mind on supper and a place to stay. "How much farther to Charleston? Is that where we are staying?"

"About twenty k's. Maybe more."

She waited before asking him something else. "We're not still going to try and find the church, are we?"

"We'll see."

"Gregg . . ."

"Heather, I love you, more than anyone, more than myself. I don't want anything to happen to you, to me, to us. But I've got to help these people. We're down here with a load of Bibles. I don't think God wants us to take them home with us."

"I know," she apologized, "but what if . . .?"

"Let's keep asking the Lord to lead us," Gregg interrupted.

Gregg glanced at the mirror again, and this time Heather saw him.

"Oh, love! Is someone following us?"

"I think so," he admitted. By now he could recognize the two headlights and the two driving lights set lower on the front of the car in back of them.

"Have they been with us for very long?"

"I don't know."

On the outskirts of Charleston they pulled into a self-service gas station. The other car came in too, until it almost touched the rear bumper of the wagon. It was the purple van.

Gregg got out and went through the ritual of lifting off the nozzle and starting the flow of gas into his tank. He was determined not to show his feelings. Planning his moves, he shut off the nozzle and hung it back on the pump, then calmly looked back at the van.

To his amazement, he saw the blonde and her sandy-haired boyfriend (or fellow agent or whatever) he had seen on the capitol steps.

Gregg could hardly manage to replace the gas cap on the Volvo. He hoped the people behind him couldn't see his hand shaking. As he turned toward the cashier's booth, the man got out of the van and came around to the pumps.

Forcing himself to remain casual, Gregg paid the girl at the window and took the coupon she handed him with his change. Behind him he could still hear the sound of the gasoline pump. Taking a chance, he took his pen from his shirt pocket, drew the half arc of the fish on the coupon, and gave it back to the girl.

The girl's eyes widened. She quickly scribbled across the paper and gave it back to Gregg. He stuffed the coupon into his jacket pocket as he got back into the car.

Gregg tried to put as much distance between himself and the van as possible, but a red light brought them to a sliding stop. Before the green came, the van pulled up immediately behind.

On the move again, Gregg cautiously drew the crumpled coupon out of his pocket and handed it to Heather. "See what this says."

Heather opened the door on the glove compartment and held the paper up to the faint light. She saw Gregg's half fish, but there was something more.

"It says, '8:30 here.' "

"That's all?"

"That's all."

"That must be what time she gets off. Let's see, it's almost seven now. She must want us to meet her."

"Gregg, we're not coming back, are we?"

"Sure, we'll come back. She's a Christian and 8:30 is when she gets off work."

"I could have read it wrong. It could be 830 Herr Street. It could be anything."

"Let's stick to our first idea. We go someplace and kill an hour and a half, then come back at 8:30."

"What about the people following us?"

"They have to eat, too," Gregg laughed. "Besides, they might get bored and go someplace else."

Heather shut her eyes, trying to ignore the knot in her stomach.

Thursday night, December 27

Brightly lit, the capitol was more beautiful now than during
the afternoon, glistening snow accentuating the soft pink and
white stonework.

The scene was lost to the Volvo driver and his
companion, however. Gregg drove as fast as he dared
through downtown. He glanced again at the dashboard
clock. 2012. He had to get rid of that van, quickly.

His heart pounded as if it were in a contest with the
wipers. If only the signal lights would cooperate. Somehow
he had to lose that wolf on his trail. Beyond the underpass
Gregg started looking for an escape route. Not this road,
nor this one. Without warning Gregg turned right, up a hill,
and floored the accelerator. The wagon skidded around the
turn and went up the hill, gaining speed. Gregg had to fight
the steering wheel to keep the car in a straight line.

Unprepared, the van driver hit the brakes and jerked the
wheel to the right, throwing the big metal box into a skid
around the turn, over the curb, and onto the sidewalk.
Driving lights smashed as bumper and frame met in an
explosion of steel and glass.

Furious, the driver powered his way back onto the road
and up the hill toward the lights of the white wagon, quickly
disappearing in the thickening snow.

Gregg noticed the amber lights were gone as his pursuers

came after him up the hill, farther away now but still gaining. He made a quick right, then a left, uphill again. Heather screamed as a group of children with sleds scattered like sparrows. One lad rolled off into the snow, his riderless sled hurtling down toward the Volvo.

Gregg swerved to miss the boy just as the sled shot between the wheels. Further down the road, the oncoming van hit it squarely, dashing the sled into a shower of splinters and torn metal.

At the top Gregg made another right. The road dropped away like a carnival slide, long and narrow and gently bent in the middle, with a severe right at the bottom. Behind them the van lights were gaining.

Gregg slammed down on the accelerator. Heather braced both feet against the firewall with her hands against the dash. The car leaped ahead. Sixty-five k's. Seventy. Seventy-five. Gregg jammed the brakes hard, then off, then hard again. He flicked the wheel to the right and the rear end started sliding. Back to the left with the wheel. Not so much. There, again. Now the power. He jammed the selector into second and floored the pedal.

"Come on, baby," he yelled.

The car skidded sideways toward a low stone wall. Heather shut her eyes and stiffened for the crash. But the tires caught and they raced over a little rise and down again toward the main street, with no lights behind them. Nothing.

It was 8:37 before they reached the gas station. The lights were out. Gregg thought they might be too late, but then he saw the girl standing in the shadows alongside the building. She got in quickly and they drove off.

"Which way?" Gregg asked.

"Back toward town."

Her name was Debbie Smith, and she was surprised to meet two people from Canada traveling in West Virginia. She directed Gregg onto the Interstate and off again at South Charleston.

"How would you have come all this way by yourself?" Gregg asked her.

"My Daddy. But I called Mom and told her I had a way."

"Did you tell her who it was?"

"No, but she knows it must be someone from church."

"That qualifies us," laughed Gregg. "We're church, all right. Would someone from the church ordinarily pick you up on Thursdays?"

Debbie answered hesitantly. "Yes. Sometimes."

"Are there services tonight?"

Debbie didn't answer, so Gregg let the subject drop. She took them to a little frame house on a back street in South Charleston. Gregg hoped he wouldn't **have** to find his way back by himself. He could see the girl's mother looking out the back window, trying to identify the car and the two strangers coming across the yard.

Debbie began the introductions once they were inside the little entryway at the back of the house. "Mom, this is Gregg and this is Heather." Looking past her mother, she asked, "Is Dad still here or did he go already?"

Her mother made no answer. "Won't you come in," she said to her guests. "No, don't worry about tracking in. The snow's clean. Leave your boots on."

But Gregg had already slipped out of his wet boots, and Heather followed his example. Mrs. Smith led them into the front room, not much larger than the kitchen.

"Call me Ann," she said, offering them places on the sofa. She had difficulty concealing her uncertainty at having two strangers suddenly drop out of nowhere.

"Let me tell you who we are," Gregg began. "Heather and I are on our Christmas holidays. We came down to visit my parents in Ohio. That's one reason we came. We also want to do anything we can to help our brothers and sisters."

He stopped, hoping Mrs. Smith would take the cue, but she did not.

"We have been praying that the Lord would lead us to the people He wants us to meet and open up the way for us to do whatever we can for them."

Ann Smith was unconvinced. She looked at Debbie, then

at Gregg again. "And you happened to meet each other?"

Debbie spoke up. "He came to the station and bought gas. And he drew a fish."

"I made the sign," Gregg said to Mrs. Smith. "You know."

"Yes."

Gregg went on. "When Debbie got off work, we met her. And here we are."

Heather felt the woman's unspoken anxiety and said to Gregg, "We should go. We don't want to cause any trouble."

How could they break through this woman's suspicions? Gregg got up to leave. His voice was gentle as he said his good-byes.

"Mrs. Smith, we must go. Before we do, I want to wish you the best, God's best. May the Lord bless you and keep you, and may He give you and your family peace."

Ann Smith said nothing, her eyes downcast as she rose out of her chair to see the strangers to the door.

Gregg added, "Could you use a Bible? We have several out in the car."

Before she could speak, Gregg heard a scraping noise behind him and turned to see a man, evidently Mrs. Smith's husband, opening the bedroom door and coming into the room. A slightly built man, his dark eyes held an almost haunted look. "Forgive me," he said, "but I heard you say you had Bibles?"

"Yes."

"I'm Robert Smith." He held his hand out to Gregg. "Do you have many you can leave us?"

"How many do you need?"

Those intense eyes scrutinized Gregg. "Do you have twenty? If you can't spare that many, leave us as many as you can."

Gregg laid his hand on the man's thin shoulder. "I can leave you 100 if you can use them."

Smith couldn't believe this was real. "A hundred?"

"I have that many and more, Mr. Smith."

"Just call me Robert." He seemed suddenly to come to life. "Are they in the car?"

"Yes."

"Debbie," her father said to the girl, "you get the car out so, so . . ., what is your name?"

"Gregg."

". . . so Gregg can put his car in the garage." Then, to Gregg, "How long will it take to get them out?"

"Five minutes," Gregg answered, "once we're in the garage, and I don't need any lights."

Smith looked at his watch, then at Gregg again. "May I ask you a question?"

"Certainly."

"Were you followed here tonight?"

"No."

Smith hesitated. "Are you sure?"

"Absolutely," Gregg responded, grinning. "There's three mirrors on that car out there, and I drive with all three, if you know what I mean."

"Good. Good." Smith rubbed his hands together. He almost didn't say it, then went ahead and asked Gregg, "May I invite you to a meeting tonight?"

"To church?"

"I don't think there will be any problems, but we can never be sure. If you would rather not come, I understand."

Gregg glanced at Heather. "We'll be glad to."

Debbie had already gone out, so Gregg quickly followed her and backed the car around and into Smith's garage. He had two full grocery sacks ready when the others came out.

Gregg got into the back seat with Heather and Debbie. Mr. Smith drove.

Gregg could see little. Smith's head and shoulders and the headrest blocked most of the front view, and the side windows were steamed over. Gregg felt trapped and helpless, and for an instant regretted having committed himself to this stranger taking him toward some unknown.

Smith finally stopped on a side street, next to a laundromat. "We'll walk from here," he said.

Smith and his wife led the way, Debbie and the two guests behind. Each of the men carried a grocery sack. Gregg felt as if he had a time bomb as the wet snowflakes peppered the heavy paper. It was all he could do to keep from looking over his shoulder to see if they were being followed.

They came to an intersection. There were no cars coming, no sign of anyone about, though there were several lights along the street. The Smiths did not cross directly, but angled off to the right across a yard, between two houses.

"Right through there," Debbie whispered, with a gesture toward the narrow opening through which her parents had disappeared.

"Here." Debbie stepped inside a dark doorway and Heather followed. Gregg bumped into Heather and almost knocked her down the stairs. All five of them were crowded onto a small landing between the basement and the upstairs.

"Sorry," Gregg said, trying to keep his balance. He had hold of someone's arm.

"Shhh."

"Sorry," he said again instinctively. Fortunately, this time he remembered to whisper.

"This way." Smith took Heather's hand and led her downstairs. Gregg, last, eased the door closed and followed the others.

The basement was divided into two rooms. Smith led them through the first and into the family room beyond. Taking his cue from Smith, Gregg left his sack of Bibles in the first room, over to one side in the darkness. Their coming interrupted a meeting in progress in the dimly lit room.

"Hello, Robert, Ann, Debbie." The greetings ended abruptly as people saw two strangers following the Smiths.

"These are friends," Robert said quickly. "This is Gregg and Heather."

"Hello."

"Welcome."

The newcomers found places on chairs or the floor. Heather counted sixteen others present besides themselves and the Smiths. A young man not much older than Gregg seemed to be in charge, and he resumed talking as soon as everyone was situated.

"We have a duty, you see. We must shine as lights in a dark place. We must live apart from the world, even while we are in the world. We cannot become bitter, and we must strive never to be discouraged.

"Our task is not to avenge ourselves, not to vindicate ourselves, but to live righteously, godly, and soberly in this present time. God has preserved His church through many dark periods in history. He has never failed us, nor will He fail us now."

Several "Amens" followed his remarks. For a moment no one said anything, then the leader spoke again.

"Welcome, brother and sister, into our little fellowship."

"Thank you."

"Are you from the city?"

"They're from out of town," put in Smith quickly.

"I see," the leader responded. "Then a special welcome to you. You picked a bad night to be on the road."

"Yes," Gregg admitted. He wondered what this sober young man would say if he knew these two strangers were from Canada and had no place to register for the night. Most of the motels would be off limits by now, their "no vacancy" signs hung out so tired desk clerks could go to bed.

"Robert"—the leader turned to Mr. Smith—"is there anything you want to say? We thought you might not be coming tonight."

"No, you go ahead. I'm glad these friends could come and be with us, and I wanted them to meet all of you and you to meet them."

The leader accepted that and moved into the final phase of the meeting. "Let's pray together before we leave. What special requests do we want to lay before the Lord?"

As she listened to the recital of names and needs from various sectors of the room, Heather found herself weeping silently. There seemed to be more requests than individuals to make them: to remember brother Kidwell, and his health; for his wife, Alice; for several who were ill; for two men who needed employment; for several young people.

Gregg's eyes, too, were wet. There were so many needs, so many requests.

". . . for Victor, that he will not become discouraged, and for his family while he is away."

". . . for Todd and Mary, that they will be able to stand firm despite the loss of his work."

". . . for Ray, and for Adrienne as she is alone now."

". . . for Jess and Luke as they come to trial, and for their wives and children, that they will be given strength."

". . . for Mary Agnes, that her baby will be healthy and that Bill will be able to stand fast during their separation."

". . . and we want to ask God again about a building."

"Yes," another voice agreed. "And constantly be praying about our registration, that it may be granted if it's the Lord's will."

"Yes," came several murmured voices.

Gregg spoke up. "And for Bill and Jan Lambert and their three children." Instantly he could tell he had said too much. He hoped the dim light concealed his embarrassment. Heather glanced around the room, trying to see what was wrong. The leader brought the requests to a close.

"And now let's go to the Lord."

To Gregg it seemed natural to kneel, although he never did back home except in his private prayers. With a minimum of movement everyone slipped out of their chairs or rose from their places on the floor and knelt in varying positions around the room.

Not everyone prayed. Not aloud, at least. With no seeming order or arrangement, different ones offered expressions of adoration, praise, and petition. To Gregg it felt as if God were right there, face to face.

Gregg opened his eyes and looked across the huddled forms, some bowed nearly to the floor, others on one knee or resting their elbows in a chair or on the divan. One young mother had her eyes open, too, her hands upraised toward heaven.

Then the leader brought the prayers to a close, with numerous "Amens" following his own.

People helped each other to their feet and expressed words of blessing and concern as they prepared to go. Coats were taken from the pile, and in twos and threes the group disbanded.

Smith made no move to go, so Gregg hung back too, shaking hands and exchanging farewells with those on their way out.

Gregg saw Smith go over and exchange a few words with
the leader. He could tell they were speaking about him.
Then Robert motioned him over.

"Gregg, I want you to meet Tim. He is our leader, now
that Brother Kidwell is away for a while. Tim is glad to
hear about those groceries in the other room."

Tim grabbed Gregg's hand and pumped it vigorously.
"Yes, brother, you've brought good news to us."

"We'll just leave them where they are," Robert cautioned
Gregg, "and Tim can take care of them from here."

"Yes," Tim agreed, "we'll certainly see that they are
placed in the hands of those who can use them best."

"There are 100 in two bags," Smith told Tim.

"A hundred! That's great," Tim said, grabbing Gregg's
hand again.

Smith had a question for Tim. "Tim, what about Matt
Ellison?"

"Ellison? You mean, have Gregg talk with him?"

"What do you think?"

"And get his opinion?" Tim asked.

"That's what I had in mind."

Gregg felt distinctly uncomfortable, totally unaware of
what these two men were talking about, yet knowing it
somehow concerned him.

"We'll talk about it in the car," Smith told him. Then, to
Tim, "We must go."

Moments later the five of them were tramping through
the snow toward Smith's car. This time Smith had Gregg sit
in the front.

"Matthew Ellison," Smith explained, "is one of the local
big shots in politics, or was. He really came to the front
during the changeover. Had his picture in the papers, that
sort of thing.

"Last spring he started coming to church. That was before
we lost our building. No one knew what to think. We all
knew where he stood. Brother Kidwell continued to preach.
He was nervous, especially at first, but then we kind of got
used to Matt and didn't pay much attention to him."

"Was he sent to observe?"

"That's what we didn't know. And still don't," Smith
explained. "He came and wanted to be baptized. That was

about the time our building was being taken, and they were preparing the case against Brother Kidwell. We were in a quandary."

"Did you baptize him?"

"No, we didn't. You see, before we can baptize we have to get a permit, supposedly for health and welfare reasons. The local Board issues the permit."

"I can't believe it."

"You can see why we didn't want to go downtown and file for a permit to baptize Matt Ellison. That would be waving a red flag in front of a mad bull."

"There are other ways to baptize," Gregg suggested.

"We know all about that, you can be sure. But suppose we go ahead and baptize this fellow at night and he's not genuine. We've already lost our building. This would be the perfect excuse to close us down altogether."

"Aren't you officially closed now?"

"Actually, no, not yet. They know we are still meeting. They even know where, on Sundays at least. There are few secrets in the D.R.A."

"And they still let you meet?"

"You could say that. We meet, but without official registration. Though they know we're meeting, and though we've repeatedly petitioned for registration, they won't give it to us. Our situation is shaky, very shaky."

"I see."

"We're just thankful for each service we have. But when this question arose about Matt, we didn't know how to handle it."

As they pulled into the drive, Smith noticed he was almost out of gas.

"We can take my car," Gregg volunteered. "Heather can go, too." Gregg correctly sensed that she would not want to be separated from him.

On the way, Gregg had a question for Smith. "What did I say wrong about Bill and Jan Lambert?"

His host tried to explain. "You didn't say anything wrong. It's just that the Lambert situation was such a front page thing, with so much publicity. Everyone immediately linked you with trouble. Lambert . . . publicity . . . trouble. Can you see the connection?"

"Sure."

"If I could offer a suggestion," Smith ventured, "could I suggest that you avoid trading names and addresses back and forth. Don't tell me where you're going from here; and don't tell the next people you meet about us. That way, if someone's forced into a situation where he or she has to answer questions, they would have no answer to give, because they don't know."

Gregg's watch showed 2248. Twelve minutes before eleven, and still no place to stay the night.

Matt Ellison turned out to be a giant of a man with a face like Beowulf. At first impression he looked like the snarling kind, but as time wore on he came across as a man whose craggy exterior overlaid an inner core of smoothly controlled power.

His home lay at the end of a country lane, a low rambling ranch house. Gregg had never expected to find this much flat ground anywhere near Charleston.

Ellison received them in his den, wearing silk pajamas and robe. The room was what Gregg had always dreamed about in his wildest imagination: walls paneled in knotty pine, a fireplace at one end of the room, knickknacks tastefully arranged on the ample bookcase.

"I joined forces with them because I felt they had the answers," Ellison explained, telling Gregg about his background, "but I was soon disillusioned. They talked equality, but they were getting extras under the table. Unlimited expense accounts, special privileges. They were on a free ride with the people shouldering the burden.

"I have these things, too, so I know what I'm talking about. But these are not the answer, nor are their slogans. I became nauseated with our propaganda phrases we spread everywhere. And our glorious programs were always more hot air than anything else. All rhetoric and no reality."

"When did you first become interested in the church?" Gregg asked.

"The church?" His words boomed across the room. Gregg thought surely they would awaken the entire household. "I've never been taken up with the church. The church is people. My concern is with a Person, the Lord.

"Last April we closed a church and confiscated their

Bibles. I kept one for myself. I used to have a Bible, but when the change came I disposed of it, as did a lot of other fringe church people. What did I care? I never read it.

"This Bible I took from the church intrigued me. I started reading at random. Perhaps a chapter in Proverbs—that's a fascinating collection. Or I would read in Genesis, or the Psalms. Then somehow I began on Luke. Luke captivated me. Next, I read the entire New Testament. I did this at night or in the car when I was by myself. I couldn't afford to have anyone see me."

"And so you decided to find a church?"

"Yes. And here I am."

"What made you want to be baptized?"

"Baptism will be my personal Rubicon. After that there'll be no turning back. I'll put myself into what Jesus did for me with His dying and burial and resurrection. My baptism will be my final step in giving my life to Christ."

"Why don't you obtain a permit?"

"I think I am more willing than is the church, although I know that my requesting permission could cause publicity and more problems for them."

"Why don't you wait until you can apply?"

"I've waited too long already. I don't want to wait any longer."

"Isn't there someone who can baptize you?"

"Who would it be? I can't ask any of my friends, of course. Nobody at the church wants anything to do with it. I feel as Paul did when they thought he was still Saul the persecutor."

Suddenly Matt's face brightened. "You baptize me, Gregg."

"Me?"

"Sure. Why not?"

"I've never baptized anyone. I'm not a preacher."

"Do you have to be? You could baptize me right now."

To Gregg that seemed even more preposterous. He thought of the snow still falling, of the fact that he and Heather were still homeless for the night, of the danger he would be placing himself and Heather in should this entire drama be a skillfully contrived trap. He had to find a way out. Then again, if Matt had really come to Christ, how could he refuse? He thought of the many encouragements he had given Heather to trust the Lord to take care of them.

He looked at Heather, at Smith, at Matt. "Okay," he told him. "I'll be glad to."

Matt sprung out of his chair and grabbed his new friend in a crushing bear hug. "Brother, you'll make me a happy man." He started to leave the room. "I want to wake up Golda. She's got to see this. I'll get some clothes for you. They'll be too big, but that won't matter."

Gregg couldn't tell whether Ellison's wife was aloof, hostile, or half-asleep. She didn't say two words beyond responding to the introductions.

"We can't go to the river," Matt warned. "Not with the patrols. Let's go to Alum Creek. It's not that far, and the snow's not coming down that badly. We'll make it back up the hill."

Gregg offered a further suggestion. "Could we take your car, too? This will give us more room, and we'll have two cars in case one gets stuck." He had another thought which he kept to himself.

On the way, Smith gave Gregg some advice. "I don't want to tell you what to do, but I think I can help you with this baptism."

Gregg kept his eyes on the taillights of Ellison's car as he listened. "Sure, go ahead."

"Turn off your heater. The outside air won't seem so cold, then. And when we get there, look for a pole of some kind, so you can test the depth."

Gregg formed the picture at once. "So I don't step into a place that's too deep?"

"Yes, that's it."

Except for their Volvo and Ellison's Buick, the road was deserted. Once at their destination, Gregg changed in the back seat, shivering as much from excitement as from the knowledge that he would soon be bitterly cold. He instructed Heather to keep the motor running and to turn the heater on full.

Out of the car, he groped for a stick, found one, and

stumbled downhill, Ellison close behind him. At the water's edge Gregg slipped out of his coat and handed it to Robert. Matt's wife refused to get out of their car, but Gregg could see her looking out the side window.

Gregg slowly exhaled as he stepped into the water, but the shock still nearly paralyzed him. Shivering, he probed in front of him with the stick and forced himself out deeper and deeper into the icy stream. Inwardly he prayed he would be able to speak, to say the baptismal words.

Matt followed Gregg out into the water. The faint light from the headlights filtered down through the falling snow as Gregg raised his right hand. His voice echoed oddly in the stillness, even above the noise of the stream.

"Matt Ellison, because you want to follow Jesus as God's Son and your personal Savior, I baptize you in the name of the Father and of the Son and of the Holy Spirit. Amen."

Matt gasped as he came out of the water, then he raised his voice in a loud "Praise the Lord," the sound booming back from the hills. He grabbed Gregg in another colossal bear hug.

"Let's get out of the water," Gregg said through chattering teeth. Ellison did not seem to know he was cold.

Shivering violently, Gregg took his coat from Smith and asked him, "Where does this road go?"

"Well, if you follow it far enough you'll get to Huntington."

"Then I'm on my way."

"But . . ."

Gregg cut short the protest. "We're on our way. May the Lord bless you. We'll pray for you. Pray that we get through."

Smith tried to hold him back. "But the weather, the snow. That road's bad enough in the daylight. There won't be any plows out and . . ."

But Gregg was already in the car, stripping off the wet clothes and throwing them out the window and putting on his own. He rammed the selector into gear and made a quick U-turn. At the bridge, instead of heading back toward Charleston he turned left.

"Love, where are we going?"

"We're getting out of here."

"What about Mr. Smith?" Heather asked, alarmed by her husband's behavior.

"Matt can take care of him."

"Where *are* we going?" she asked again, her voice rising.

"If that guy's sincere," Gregg answered, "he's a Christian. If he's not, then we're getting as far away from this place as we can."

"Gregg," she screamed, "where are we going? We can't go this way."

"Sure we can," he told her, pressing harder on the accelerator. "Look. There are tire tracks to follow. This is a good road."

She leaned forward and tried to make out the roadway as it wound through the last of the little settlement. The curving, crooked surface was snow-covered and visibility was nearly zero, but Gregg was right. There were tracks. Other cars had gone this way. She sat back and tried to remain calm, wishing he would at least slow down.

Farther on they came to a fork in the road. Following his intuition, Gregg turned right. They had not gone far before both he and Heather realized this was not the same.

The snow was coming harder and now there were no tracks.

Friday morning, December 28

The pulsating idle of a semi woke Heather with a start. For one panic moment she couldn't remember where she was.

"Hey, sleepyhead," Gregg said gently, "we're here."

Heather sat up. "Where is here?"

"A truck stop, just outside Huntington."

"What are we doing next?" she asked, feeling for her boots and reaching around for her coat.

"Let's have a coffee," Gregg answered, pulling on his coat. "It's too early to cross."

"What time is it?" Heather asked, stifling a yawn as she

answered her own question. The dashboard clock showed
530, but by appearances it could have been midnight. The
world ended in blackness beyond the parking lot lights. It
was still snowing hard.

Gregg didn't seem in any hurry to get out of the car.
"I'm glad you were able to sleep. You needed it."

"Love, I'm so glad to be over that awful road."

"Pretty bad, wasn't it?"

"Gregg, let's not do that again tonight. I couldn't take
it."

He misread her shiver. "Let's go in where it's warm."

The brisk air cleared away Heather's sleepiness.
"Hey"—Gregg leaned closer to his wife as he sat across
from her—"you're pretty."

She smiled.

"You're always good-looking when you first wake up."

Heather wrinkled her nose at him and started to answer,
but the waitress intruded. She looked as if she could drive a
bulldozer. She laid her order pad on the table. "Breakfast?"

Gregg could hardly hear over the loud wail of the radio.
He asked Heather, "Would you like to have ham and
eggs?"

"Only one, I think," she answered. "One egg, over
lightly. May I have tea?"

"Toast?" The girl's chipped fingernails wore bright pink
polish. If either one of the diamonds on her left hand were
genuine, she was worth more than the restaurant.

"Yes, please. And whole wheat, if you have it."

The waitress turned to Gregg. "You?"

"Ham and two eggs. Toast. Coffee."

"Ham?" She looked at Heather.

"No, thank you."

"Wow," Gregg said sarcastically as the pained nasal voice
on the radio droned on.

"You'd be short too, love, if you'd worked all night."

He grinned at her. "What do you think I did?"

Involuntarily Heather shuddered again. "I know. I'll be
glad when we . . . " She was interrupted by the waitress
again.

"This'll warm you up," the girl said as she set two

steaming cups on the table. The poor wretch on the radio seemed in agony. Mercifully, the song ended.

Heather daintily dangled her tea bag in the clear liquid and watched the dark stain dye the water. Gregg kept his eyes on her face and hands. *Lord, keep her safe.* Feeling his stare, she flushed.

Across the room a group of truckers finished their breakfast, punctuating their loud talk now and then with laughter.

"What time do you want to . . . you know?" Heather asked.

"Whenever we get through here," he answered, checking his watch. "I don't want to get there before 6:30 or 7:00. I hope there'll be a string of workers crossing, or truck traffic, or something like that."

Gregg went at his breakfast with gusto, but Heather ate more slowly, picking at her food. By the time they had finished and were back in the car the clock showed 6:10. The morning was still pitch black.

"Are we early now, love?"

"About right," Gregg answered. "It'll take us probably fifteen or twenty minutes to get there."

The Volvo mixed with the morning flow of inbound traffic, slowed by a timid soul groping along up ahead.

"Sure glad we're not in a hurry," Gregg said to the slim figure beside him.

Heather noticed Gregg was checking the mirrors frequently. Before she could ask, he answered, "There's nobody back there. There's a string of cars, but nobody's interested in us."

"I'm glad for that."

"The thing is, when we're being followed, at least we know where they are. This way, we don't know what to think."

"What about the border, love?"

Gregg didn't answer immediately. "I don't know. I've never crossed here before. I only went into Kentucky once before, from Cincinnati. It wasn't bad then. Wasn't bad on the way back, either."

"Is Kentucky as strict?"

"Not like here. Anyplace is easier than West Virginia."

The big green and white Interstate sign was coming into view. Gregg took the westbound ramp. At once traffic thinned out, a long string of cars continuing toward the city. The Interstate was cleared, the right lane at least, and suddenly they were alone. Heather sensed Gregg's tenseness.

"Do you wish there were more cars?"

"Yes. That would make it easier."

"What if they ask us where we stayed last night?"

Gregg had forgotten all about that. "Let's hope they don't."

"Gregg, do you think they will?"

"Hon"—he spoke sharply—"just relax, and keep praying."

They rounded a gentle left turn and were at the checkpoint. They had no time to prepare themselves. Beyond the floodlit plaza lay an enormous refinery. There were no cars ahead of them.

"Keep praying." Gregg's voice was grim.

Gregg stopped the car and handed their documents across to a silent figure in the booth. Three men and a woman crowded together inside the tiny cubicle, all in green uniforms. Two of the men were engrossed in conversation with the woman, while the man who had accepted their papers was busy counting the contents of a cash drawer.

Trying not to be obvious, Gregg leaned over until he could see into the booth. He noticed that their papers were lying on the shelf beside the woman. She evidently had not seen them laid there, nor had either of the two men with her. The third man had finished his counting and was copying numbers on a slip of paper.

Gregg moved the dashboard clock ahead a couple of minutes to match the clock on the outside of the booth. Three minutes before seven. He and Heather said nothing to each other.

Finished with his counting, the man turned and spoke to one of his companions. With a quick motion he opened the door and started out, nearly colliding with Gregg's door in the process.

Surprised, he caught himself, then stopped and said something to one of the two who had just come on duty. Gregg missed what he said, but did manage to hear the reply.

"No, you take care of them. They're yours."

"Look, man, I'm off duty now, and I still have to go to the office."

"Finish your shift. They're yours."

The first man reached back into the booth and picked up Gregg's papers. Turning back to Gregg, he asked, "What do you need?"

"Could we have a transit pass?"

The officer nodded, went inside the booth, stamped the forms, and handed them back. Gregg paid him, and the officer waved the car through the barrier.

Beyond the crossing point the roadway opened onto a high, long bridge. Gregg started to comment about the refinery, but then he saw the guards.

"What is this?" he said under his breath.

Heather was not even looking at the refinery. Her attention was focused on the two solemn guards patrolling the bridge, side by side.

"They're sure protecting this place," Gregg muttered. "Not much of a crossing, though. The Lord answered our prayers."

"Did you have an idea it would be this way, love?"

"No, but He did."

"We're not going to drive all night again, are we?"

"No," he promised. "I hope not. Tonight we need to register anyway." He paused, then, "You know that crossing was so fast, I wonder if he even put us into the computer."

"Would it make any difference?"

"Not to me, that's for sure."

"What if he didn't?"

"Then he didn't. We have to register tonight, no matter what. I don't want two nights on our visas without a stamp and a place."

"I'd like to have a tub of really hot water."

"I'll get you warm," he said, reaching for her.

She took his hand and placed it back on the steering wheel. "You drive, love."

"We need to contact Ian, too," Gregg remembered.

"Whom are we planning to see here?"

"An older couple, Josh and Lula Crittenden. You'll like them."

"Are there many churches in Kentucky?"

"I think so. There used to be, from what I hear. We could try to make some other contacts between here and Lexington."

The four-lane highway unwound in gentle curves through the scrubby hills, with more snow coming down in steady sheets across the road. Heather was already dozing again.

Fresh tracks in the median told Gregg that this road had been treacherous last night, too. Dark streaks showed where a car had spun off; then more streaks and mud indicated where a tow truck had pulled out the stranded motorist.

Gradually the morning became light. On the left they passed a perfect model for Heather's sketch pencil—an unpainted cabin made out of hand-hewn logs, the chimney made out of field stone. Smoke from the chimney indicated someone lived there. But Gregg felt he shouldn't disturb Heather's rest.

Gregg drove with one eye on the rear view mirror, but as far as he could tell they were alone. About an hour west of the crossing, a dull-colored sedan gradually overtook them and settled into a steady position a little ways back.

The sedan was too far away for Gregg to make out any details. There seemed to be two people in the front seat, and he was able to make out a dark shape on the dash behind the windshield. Gregg strained to see what it was, but hesitated to slow his speed enough for the car behind to overtake them. The shape on the dash must be some kind of instrument, maybe a long-range camera.

He tensed when the sedan pulled out and started to pass, then relaxed with a laugh, waking up Heather.

"What is it?" she asked, rubbing her eyes.

"I thought this car was following us," he explained. "I could see two people in the front and thought sure it was two cops."

"But it wasn't?"

"There was this black thing on the dashboard. I thought it was a box or maybe a camera. They were so far back I couldn't get a good look. When she passed, it was a woman with a kid and the black thing was the kid's teddy bear."

"Love," Heather told him, "you've been doing this work too long."

"Do you think we'll be able to find the Crittendens?" Heather asked a moment later.

"I hope so," Gregg answered. "I'd like to find some new people, too."

"What if we're not able to?"

"There must be churches all through these hills."

Gregg's confidence proved mistaken. At the next exit they made another stop for coffee and tea. Greg drew his little diagram as he paid the check, but the waitress only gave him a blank stare.

He tried the gas station alongside the coffee shop but there again, he drew the sign with no result. No response at the next exit, either, from the waitress in the restaurant nor the boy who sold Gregg the gas and quart of oil.

"I hope we find someone soon," Heather commented as Gregg pulled away from the station. "I've had my fill of tea."

"I've got coffee coming out of my ears," he agreed. "We'll find somebody."

"You sound so definite."

"There's got to be someone in Lexington."

Rolling fields stretched on either side of the highway. To their left a rambling mansion graced a knoll.

"Look, love," Heather said, pointing. "Isn't that lovely?"

"Hey," Gregg responded, "think of what that place looks like in the summer."

"Are these farms?"

"Tobacco farms, maybe?" he answered. "I'll bet those barns back there are where they dry their tobacco."

Beyond a little rise they saw the flashing lights of a patrol car, sitting behind a panel delivery truck. The driver had the back doors of the truck opened, and the officer was questioning him.

"Glad he wasn't after us," Gregg admitted once they were past.

"They're everywhere, aren't they, Gregg?"

"Everywhere. Such a great country—such a tragedy."

At Lexington Gregg tried again. At the exit he pushed his way through the snow past the first gas station and its matching restaurant, silently praying for guidance. He turned in at an orange sign and rolled down his window.

"I don't need gasoline yet," he began, hesitant to disclose his purpose. The attendant was a round-faced fellow who looked harmless enough. Gregg decided to go ahead. "We're passing through," he said, "and we thought maybe you could tell us where there's a church."

The bland face stared at Gregg a moment, then spoke. "Right on Broadway. You can't miss it. Go down this street past the Belt Line, all the way downtown. Broadway and Second. You can't miss it. That's the only church left around here."

They had no trouble spotting the massive brick structure. Gregg parked the car, and the two of them got out. No one seemed to pay them any attention as they crossed the street and walked uphill toward the old building.

Gregg found the brisk wind and the snow exhilarating. "You know what?" he said to Heather. "I'm having fun."

She looked up at him, then said, "I like being with my husband. I wish he wouldn't frighten me with his adventures, but I like being with him."

All the time they had been within sight of the church, Gregg had not seen anyone either enter or leave it. Now that they were closer, he could see there were no footprints leading up to the front door.

The door was locked. Gregg half turned to see whether anyone on the street was watching, then knocked. Heather forced herself to stand still. Cold, she wanted to stamp her feet or jump up and down. Or run; surely people were staring.

Gregg took off his glove and knocked again, the dull sound echoing through the empty building.

"Love"—she tugged at his arm—"let's go."

"Let's try around back."

She didn't want to, but they tried every door. The locked building remained silent and cold.

Finally Gregg said, "Let's go find a place to eat."

"Yes, I'm ready," Heather said, more relief than appetite in her answer.

They left the car by the curb and walked. Twenty minutes and a sandwich later, they were back. Gregg's decoration on the restaurant meal check had gone for nothing, too.

"Let's not stay long, love," Heather pleaded as they passed the car with its security and privacy. She tensed as a patrol car drove by, but Gregg kept walking.

"Not so fast, love."

"I'm sorry." He slowed down.

"You're as anxious as I am. You don't think I can tell."

He grinned back at her. "Let's say, excited. I'm not nervous, just excited."

"You can be excited if you want to be," she told him. "With me, it's nervousness."

Anyone watching would have thought they were discussing plans for a party or special occasion. Their excitement lessened, however, when they came to the church and tried the door again, with no better results than before.

Gregg spotted a phone booth. "Let's see if the church has a listing. There might be a preacher's name, too."

They both crowded into the phone booth, but even with the two of them looking, they were unable to find a listing for a church or a minister.

"What do we do now, love?"

Gregg wiped his hand across his tired eyes, then put his glove back on. "We'll try Josh and Lula. We could make a run down there and then back, providing we don't stay."

"Where will we stay tonight?" she asked.

"We're running out of time. Let's see if we can make it to Cincinnati for tonight."

Friday afternoon, December 28

Bert Wilson studied the reports in front of him, grunting now and then, muttering to himself as he digested the data. "Randall, motorhome, Cambridge; Reese, Ford, Wayside Inn, Parkersburg; Richards, Volvo . . ."

He stopped short, scowled, looked at the list again, and worked his massive jaw from side to side.

"Where is that Richards?"

He turned to the console beside him and began tapping the keyboard. Still scowling as he read the flickering words, Wilson tore off the printout and reached for the phone. Minutes later he had his party on the line.

"Bellville, is that you? Wilson here. . . . Yeah, thanks. . . . Say, Stan, how come we don't have a report on a suspect car I had posted on the sheets, a white Volvo wagon, Ontario 284-BRX, believed occupied by . . ."

The voice on the other end interrupted. Wilson didn't like what he heard. "Were your people hurt? How bad? Were they able to give you anything?"

Wilson shoved the chair out of the way and stood up, shaking his finger as if Stan Bellville were there in the room.

"Keep on it, Stan. He hasn't crossed yet, so my guess is he's right there in Charleston. Keep me posted, hear?"

At that moment the Volvo in question was stopping in front of an abandoned general store south of Lexington, Kentucky. Lemaster's Store had long since seen its last customer. A hand-operated gasoline pump rusted near the far end of the sagging porch. The roof looked as if it could hardly bear the heavy layer of wet snow.

The road ended in front of Lemaster's in a turn-around between the store and two white frame church buildings a stone's throw apart on either side of a little cemetery. The one on the left had its windows broken out and the door was gone.

"Love," exclaimed Heather, "do we have time enough for me to sketch the churches and the cemetery? I must have this on paper."

"Tell you what," he answered, "I'll go see if Josh is here. You go ahead and work."

To Heather it seemed only moments before Gregg returned with a white-haired gentleman who introduced himself as Josh Crittenden.

"Shake hands with a sixty-year-old preacher," he said. Laughing at his own joke, Josh told her, "Never been sixty before. Thought I'd try it a year and see how I like it."

Gregg took charge of the conversation. "Josh says nobody's around, and we can get the Bibles out right here."

Heather had been so intent on her sketching that she did not notice where Gregg went, nor where he and Josh had come from. Surely there were other people around. They had passed two houses before coming to the store.

Josh saw her expression and answered her unspoken query. "Them's my neighbors. They won't make us any trouble. Even if they was to be watchin', they wouldn't care."

Gregg busied himself in back, the seat now folded up, stacking Bibles for his talkative friend.

"Used to be we had two churches here. They closed that one down. Said they needed space for storage. Never stored one ear of corn, not one potato, nothin'. But they got 'er closed, they did. We still got the meetin' house. An' she's full on a Sunday. You oughta stay over an' see."

Finished, Gregg stood up. On impulse he opened the

tailgate and emptied the overnighter into the big suitcase, then brought the smaller case around and filled it with the remaining Bibles. He had half a dozen or so left and handed them to Heather.

"Want to slip these in your purse?"

Remembering his previous experience, Gregg broke loose the thin framework built into the compartment and threw the pieces on the ground.

Looking at the wood scraps on the snow, he said to Josh, "I'm leaving you a few souvenirs, if you don't mind."

Josh laughed. "Son, I don't mind. What's a handful of splinters to what I got here?"

Gregg put the seat back down and replaced the suitcases, then closed the tailgate. "We have to be on our way."

"You can't stay for supper? Mom'll be disappointed."

"No, friend, we'd better not."

Seeing Gregg's determination, Josh asked, "Find your way out, can you?"

"Sure, no problem." Gregg looked over the dead-end turnaround, the rickety store building, and the two little structures across the road. "Although I admit this isn't the Interstate."

Josh laughed again. "We'll make a briar hopper outa you yet."

Gregg took the knobby hand the old man offered him, then put his arm around Josh and embraced him. "I wish we could stay, my friend," Gregg told him, "but we can't. God be with you."

Crittenden offered his hand to Heather. The three of them prayed together, then the Volvo left.

"He's one of the best, Heather."

"Is he a preacher?"

"He is now," Gregg explained. "He used to be a farmer, tenant farmer at that. When the change came there was no one to preach, so Josh started preaching himself. He preaches in that little church back there, but that old man carries Bibles all over this state. He doesn't look the part, does he? That may be one reason he can do so much. By this time next week, Josh will have every one of those Bibles out."

Heather was quietly amazed. "Just a simple old man."

This time Gregg bypassed Lexington and headed north on I-75, crowding the speed limit as much as he dared. Near the Williamstown exit they met a southbound convoy of Army vehicles, but they didn't see a single patrol car between Lexington and Cincinnati.

The road signs indicated there was an airport off to their left. The four-lane dropped in a long, steep hill to the river and the bridge. Gregg found himself boxed into the center lane behind a milk truck and a spray-slinging semi.

"If all these people are going to cross," he complained, "we'll be there all night."

At the border, the crosswind was strong enough to shake the car with each gust. But once they were on the bridge, the upper level protected them from the snow.

"My eyelids feel like sandpaper," he told his companion.

Heather had her own complaints. "I am tired, my back and shoulders hurt, and I don't think I will ever feel rested again."

"You're getting old," her husband teased.

"It's the hours we keep."

"Tonight we'll get to bed earlier," Gregg said as they inched toward the barrier.

Heather made no reply. She was sitting erect and her eyes were open, but her lips were moving. Theirs was the third car now. Gregg uttered a silent petition, too, as he watched the drama up front.

Here we go, he said to himself.

When it was their turn, Gregg moved into position and cut the ignition. The inspector stood to one side, waiting, as Gregg handed their papers across to the officer.

"Looks as if you're traveling," the man inside the booth said.

"Yes, sir. We're on holidays."

"How long will you be staying?"

"Tonight and tomorrow night. Two nights."

The officer opened both passports, looked from Gregg's face to his passport photograph, then stooped so he could see inside the car to Heather. "Looks as if you're the same people."

Half turning, he glanced at the image forming on the screen beside him and turned back to Gregg. Since Gregg had avoided looking directly at the man, he missed the slight lifting of eyebrows and the officer's smothered reflex.

"Mind if we see in your car?" His tone was as pleasant as before. He nodded to the man standing near Heather's door.

Gregg got out of the car, pulling on his coat. He lifted the tailgate and stepped out of the way for the uniformed figure, who began probing around the cargo area. Ignoring the snow, the man pointed to the two-suiter.

"Please open the suitcase."

"Yes, sir."

Gregg quickly laid the case open and watched as the man inserted his practiced hands down through the clothes, hair dryer, and toiletries. He leaned closer and carefully ran his fingers around the lining and the seams.

Satisfied, the man straightened up and tapped the right hand compartment. "What is this?"

"That's the windshield washer for the back window." Gregg pointed to the spray nozzle on the rear pillar.

"What will they think of next?" Pointing to the center compartment, he asked, "In here?"

Gregg lifted the lid and was told to close it again.

"Here?"

"That's the spare tire," Gregg answered and started to unscrew the cover.

The inspector waved him aside. "No need for that." Satisfied, he turned away.

The man inside the booth returned Gregg's papers, accepted payment for the toll and visas, and waved them through. Behind them another car pulled into place.

Inside the booth, however, the officer keyed a series of digits to alert the Midwest Office in Columbus, and the Security Patrol in Cincinnati, that Ontario Volvo 284-BRX was now in Ohio with a two-day pass. Automatically the same information was relayed to Washington.

Cincinnati's rush hour traffic moved slowly because of the snow and frequently came to a halt. Gregg finally managed to reach Hopple and cut back across the Interstate, then wound around the hill past a hospital and up Clifton.

Heather could tell he knew where he was going. He cut down a side street to the left, so he missed seeing the two-man car coming down Ludlow toward I-75.

"Look at the gas lights," he said, pointing.

"Oh, aren't they lovely," Heather said. "I've not seen them before."

A block or so down the side street, Gregg turned into a narrow driveway and parked in back of a faded stucco. From the street the car could not have been seen, even in daylight.

"You've been here before, love?"

"A couple of times. The Nelsons live here. He's a chemist, works for a big company here in town."

Gregg helped her out of the car. The path to the door looked as if it had just been shoveled.

"Greetings in the name of Jesus," Gregg said to the woman who answered their knock.

"Come in. Do come in." Her invitation was quick and genuine. "We heard you drive in. I said to Richard, anyone who is out on a night like this wants to come or they wouldn't chance the weather."

Gregg laughed. "We wanted to come, Mrs. Nelson. I wanted you to meet Heather. Heather, this is Vivian Nelson."

The two women exchanged greetings and handshakes. "Come in," urged Mrs. Nelson. "Richard will be down in a second. He just now came in from work."

Vivian Nelson took them into a comfortable living room where a fireplace provided the focal point for a couch and chairs. Heather felt at home immediately. Evidently Gregg did, too, because he plopped down into one of the chairs and was asleep almost at once.

"Gregg's tired," said Vivian, "and you must be worn out, too."

"Thank you, I'm quite all right," Heather answered. "We've been doing a great deal of driving and Gregg has had the most of it."

"Let him sleep," said Vivian, leading Heather back toward the kitchen. "Give me a hand and we'll have supper on the table in a jiffy."

When Richard Nelson came downstairs, he settled quickly

into the rocker and glanced at the newspaper while the women finished in the kitchen. He recognized Gregg, but didn't want to awaken him. Finally, Nelson could take the newspaper no longer and put it aside.

Heather came to call them to supper. Gregg, embarrassed for his bad manners, apologized, but Nelson would have none of that. "We're just glad you could take a nap," he said. "You must have needed it."

Over the meal the conversation turned to church matters. "We're getting along," Richard said, in response to Gregg's inquiry. "Because we are a city church, we have some advantages that we would not have were we outside Cincinnati."

"And some disadvantages," added Mrs. Nelson.

"Yes," her husband admitted, "Vivian is right. We talked about it when you were here before, Gregg." Nelson spoke more for Heather's benefit than for her husband's.

"The authorities know that travelers come through on their way south because of I-75. They know people stop and want to find out if there's a church in Cincinnati, and how the church is doing. So we are able to have our services with very little interference."

No one said anything, so Nelson continued.

"Many buildings have been closed, and we've had to double up in our worship. In one way that's been good. We've had to learn to get along with each other. We can't afford the differences we had before.

"But there are other problems." Nelson spoke with emphasis now. "We have no freedom to evangelize. We've had to close our youth camp at Clermont. Our seminary was merged with the state university at Columbus, and the courses assigned to the Department of Religious Affairs. That has been a source of unhappiness, believe me."

Mrs. Nelson added, "We cannot do anything to bring new people into the church. We cannot have our young people attend church camp. We can't speak a word about Jesus outside the building. We are denied literature, except for what is printed with government approval. We can't even buy a Bible. The government is doing all it can to restrict, and defeat, us."

Nelson laid down his fork. "But even now it's not as bad

as it could be, nor as difficult as it might be for us in the future."

Nelson's comments brought the conversation to a momentary halt, and for several minutes everyone ate in silence. A knock at the back door broke the spell. Both Nelson and his wife rose to answer it, but he motioned for her to remain with their guests while he went to see who had come.

Heather glanced at Gregg. They couldn't leave now, not with their car in the back driveway. Whoever was coming must already have seen the station wagon.

The voices came through the kitchen as Nelson appeared, shepherding two college boys ahead of him.

"Gregg and Heather, this is Terry," referring to the taller of the two, "and this is Rick. Rick and Terry are students at State."

"Glad to meet you."

Mrs. Nelson set two extra places and busied herself with serving. "Here, sit down."

"No, thanks, Mrs. Nelson," Terry said. "We just finished supper at my place."

Mrs. Nelson was not to be put off. "Well I never saw boys who couldn't eat chocolate cake, even if they'd had their supper."

Terry spoke for himself and Rick. "Maybe just a little piece."

"What brings you out on a night like this?" Nelson asked the boys.

They looked at each other, then Terry answered, "We've got a problem, Mr. Nelson. Rick and I have to get back to State, and we were wondering if you knew of anyone going to Columbus this weekend?"

Fear gripped Heather's stomach. She looked at her husband, but if he read her expression he gave no sign.

Nelson answered the boys. "This weekend? No, Terry, I don't. Why do you have to go back? I thought you would be on vacation until after New Year's."

"We are," answered Rick, "but I have this paper I have to finish before then, and if I don't get it done my prof said he'd drop me out of the course."

Terry cut in. "They're already making it hard for Rick on

account of his being a Christian. The prof doesn't need to have this paper, but he's making it harder on Rick just to have a reason to put him down."

Rick explained, "I wouldn't have come home, but with mother sick and its being Christmas I couldn't see staying on campus."

"What will happen if you don't have it by the deadline?" Gregg asked.

Terry answered for his friend. "If Rick doesn't get it in, then he's finished, and he needs this course. The thing is, Rick's grades are good on the tests. There's no way the prof can cut him, except for this paper. And the prof has been after him for being so open about Jesus."

Gregg was surprised. "You're able to witness on the university campus?"

"No," Rick protested, "I'm no witness. What Terry means is that they know I'm a believer. And I guess he's right about Melton being out to get me. I don't mind that, except that I need to get this paper in, because if I don't then Melton will have me for sure."

"And you'll lose the whole course?" Gregg asked.

"That's the way it is."

Gregg looked at his wife. "We're going to Columbus, and you can go with us."

Terry hesitated. "We can't ride with you. What if you're stopped?"

"What do you mean?" Heather wanted to know.

"If we're stopped," Terry explained, "they'll want to know how we happened to be riding with you, how we came to meet."

Gregg pounded his fist on the table. "They won't stop us. We'll take you."

Nelson asked the boys, "Is there any other way you can travel?"

Rick answered, "I've checked every bus going from here to Columbus to Cleveland to Dayton to Zanesville and across. I've tried everything I could think of. The only way is to hitchhike, and you know what that means."

Gregg looked at Nelson, who explained, "No one is permitted to travel without permission, so the authorities naturally suspect anyone who is hitchhiking."

"We'll take you," Gregg offered again.

Terry considered Gregg's proposal. "When would you be leaving?"

"Any time you want. Now, or tomorrow. In fact, it would be a whole lot better if we went now, so we can travel after dark." He looked at Heather, remembering their nightmare trip from Charleston and his promise to her for tonight. She sent him back a weak smile.

"I'm not packed," Terry began, "but I can see you're right about going tonight."

"I'll go along with that," Rick agreed.

Gregg rose out of his chair. "Then we go tonight."

Mr. Nelson offered his advice. "Why don't you boys go get your things together. Meanwhile, these two people can stretch out and have a short nap. Better still, let's let them sleep to about three o'clock, then you can leave and still be in Columbus before morning."

"I don't like to say it," Gregg pointed out, "but I need to have a place to register tonight. If we leave now, then we could check into a motel. Even if we get there late, we might find someplace."

Nelson studied Gregg's face. "Gregg, you're in no shape to start driving again until you've had some rest. I'll register you here. You can give me your passport numbers, and I'll take them downtown first thing in the morning."

"But won't this mean trouble for you?"

"Not that much. I can say you stopped and stayed the night and then left my place for home. I presume you are on your way to Toronto?"

"Yes, we are."

Terry stuck out his hand to Gregg. "You don't know how much this means to us, doing this for Rick."

"Don't worry about that. Glad we can help a brother. We're not to Columbus yet. Better hold your thanks."

Four hours later Mr. Nelson's summons barely penetrated Gregg's consciousness. Gregg nudged Heather until she was awake too, and they forced their groaning bodies to go through the motions of dressing and preparing again for the road.

"Are you going to leave any Bibles?" Heather whispered, reminding Gregg of those in her purse.

"No," he responded, his voice low. "Not since we have to register here."

At 3:30 in the morning Cincinnati was dark and cold. The snow had stopped, at least. In spite of her uneasiness about what they were doing, Heather fell asleep as soon as they were on the Interstate. Before long both back seat occupants were asleep, too.

Gregg played the radio softly, listening to Cincinnati's government station. He wanted to switch to short wave, but thought it better not to reveal the transceiver to strangers, even though they were fellow believers.

Hardly any cars were on the road. Trucks, mostly. One convoy in the southbound lanes numbered eleven all told, each cab tucked close behind the trailer ahead like a lighted parade of circus elephants.

Faint gray outlined the horizon as they neared Columbus. The boys were awake, but not talkative. They seemed to become more uncomfortable the closer they came to the city. Heather was awakened by Terry's voice, giving Gregg directions.

"We take 315 and go north," he said.

Now that they were coming into town, everybody sat up and kept their eyes open for patrols. The boys were ready to duck out of sight should they need to.

"What's it like at school, as a Christian?" Gregg asked.

"In some ways," Terry answered, "things are the same, minus the church."

Rick disagreed. "It makes a difference. For example, in Political Science we were discussing the Fifth Amendment, and I asked if it covered every illegality or only a certain few."

"What is the Fifth Amendment?" Heather asked.

"It's a part of our Constitution," Terry answered, "that says a guy can't be forced to give evidence that is self-incriminating."

"What did they say?" Gregg queried.

"Well," Rick hedged, "I shouldn't have asked. Now they know I'm a believer. I should have kept my mouth shut."

Terry interrupted. "We get off at the next exit."

As he mingled with the morning traffic on Lane, Gregg

finally came to a decision he had been struggling with for
the last twenty minutes. "Could you guys use a couple of
Bibles? We could give you two or three Bibles apiece if you
could use them. Maybe you know someone who'd like to
have one."

Their passengers looked at each other. Rick shook his
head, while Terry answered. "Don't get us wrong, but I
think we're going to decline. If we got caught giving out
Bibles, it would mean good-bye State for us. You know?"

"Terry and I wanted to room together," Rick added. "It
would be a big help if we were in the same room."

"Right," agreed Terry, "but they don't let you choose
who you room with."

Rick went on, "If we were able, we could do a lot of
things. But we'd better decline your offer."

"Okay."

"Thanks, brother, anyway."

"Let us out at the light," Terry directed.

The traffic signal turned red. Gregg came to a stop, and
the boys were gone.

"That was something," Gregg commented. "If I'd known
what kind of guys they were, I don't think . . ."

"Love," Heather told him, "you would have brought
them anyway."

"To think they wouldn't take a Bible." Gregg was
disgusted.

"Love, we'd best not be critical. I'm sure they would have
taken them if they had thought they could."

"You'd think," he argued, "that on a university campus
they'd want all the Bibles they could get."

Heather changed the subject by asking, "Love, do you
know if, at home, a person can be made to give evidence
against himself?"

"I don't know," he answered. "I should know, but I
don't. Makes me wonder what I'd do if it were me, now
that I think about it."

"Where do we go now, love?"

"We're going up along the lake. Lakewood, in fact. To
see a family. Then we'll go west along the lake to see a
preacher. Then home."

"I thought we were going back the way we came."

"Let's go up through Michigan and across the 401."

"Oh, Gregg, we'll be so tired."

"Hey"—he slid his fingertips up through the little curls at the nape of her neck—"believe it or not, this way we'll get across the border quicker."

"That sounds good. I vote for your way."

"How would you like to stay in Windsor tonight?"

"I'd love it."

"We can make it. We've got the whole day."

"Then let's."

"Or"—he thought a moment—"we could go see these people in Lakewood, then stop and see the old fellow at Port Clinton, and hit for Detroit and stay there and see if we could find a place to go to church tomorrow morning."

"Gregg, I thought we were going home."

"We'll get there," he consoled her. "Let's just wait and see how everything's going by tonight. Okay?"

Heather wasn't so sure. "I'm ready to go home."

"Let's wait and see."

Saturday, December 29

The Volvo passed the Mt. Gilead exit before Gregg realized they had company again. Heather caught him looking in the mirror and asked, "Gregg, is there someone following?" He nodded, his jaw set.

"Gregg,"—Heather kept her gaze straight ahead—"I don't think I can take this."

He noticed her clenched fingers. Her knuckles were white, her hands trembling. He tried to reassure her. "We'll be okay, hon. Don't worry."

Gregg finally pulled off at Mansfield. To his surprise, the car he had thought was following them continued on toward Cleveland.

"Maybe they weren't following us after all," he mused.

Heather shivered. "I hope not."

Gregg wound around the confused maze of access roads and the off ramp and started to turn in at the Red Pantry. Suddenly he had an idea. "We'll fool those guys," he said as he turned back onto the Interstate ramp.

"Love, what are we doing?"

"Now we're in back of them," he told her. "We're the ones who are following. He thinks we'll be off the road."

Gregg kept an even closer watch behind him, determined that if another car picked them up he at least wanted to know it. About an hour farther, just beyond the turnpike, a car coming southbound flashed his headlights. Gregg slowed, then picked up speed again, holding a couple of k's under the limit.

Where was the patrol car? Then Gregg saw it, partially hidden behind a crossover bridge, its timing unit aimed back at the oncoming traffic.

Half a kilometer farther the second car waited. Gregg could hear Heather's breathing as they drove past. He kept his eye on the mirror and was startled when the chase car pulled out and fell in behind them.

Heather could feel his sudden tension. "What is it?"

He didn't answer.

"Is he coming after us?"

Just then the red lights came on and Gregg's heart sank. Rigid in her seat, Heather stared straight ahead. "No, no."

Gregg motioned for her to be quiet. He eased off onto the snow-covered shoulder and came to a stop, the patrol car right behind. With maddening slowness the officer got out of the police car and came up to Gregg's open window.

"In a hurry?"

"No, sir."

"Where are you going?"

Gregg's mind worked rapidly. "Home."

"Do you live around here?" There was no way the man could have missed the Ontario license plate.

"No, we live in Canada."

"I see." Was there a hint of antagonism in the man's manner?

"May I see your driver's license?"

Gregg reached for his billfold, careful not to move too

fast. He didn't want to get shot. As he handed over his license, Gregg saw that the officer's holster had been unsnapped. Gregg wondered how many milliseconds it would take for the blue-jacketed man to draw the gun and fire.

"Do you have any other identification?"

Wordlessly, Gregg motioned for Heather to get their passports and visas. The officer took the documents, glanced at them, then walked back to his car.

Both occupants of the Volvo knew what was happening now. Out of the corner of his eye Gregg watched in the rear view mirror as the officer spoke into his hand mike, listened and spoke again, then started writing.

No longer cold, Gregg felt himself sweating as he saw the officer get out and walk up to their car again. The man handed back the papers and Gregg's license, plus a yellow ticket.

"We clocked you at 20 k's over the limit, 120 in a 100 zone."

Instinctively Gregg opened his mouth to protest, then simply said, "Yes, sir."

"Do you wish to contest this?"

Gregg had to force his reply. "No, sir."

The officer droned on. "You may appear in court, if you wish, or you may settle now. If you settle now, the fine will be forty dollars."

"Yes, sir."

Gregg took two twenties out of his billfold and gave them to the officer. He couldn't resist a parting shot. "May I have a receipt for that?"

The officer scowled. "You can have two receipts if you want, one for each twenty." He turned and walked back to his car again.

Heather started to speak, but Gregg silenced her. The officer returned, handed Gregg a receipt for the money, then motioned for them to proceed.

"Thank you."

Now that they were by themselves again, Gregg vented his anger. "A hundred and twenty in a 100 zone! That guy knows I wasn't going that fast. Well, he got what he wanted. He looked us over. Forty bucks shot, too."

Heather tried to calm him. "At least the boys weren't with us. And we had the money."

"Another time or two like that and we won't have the money. He had no right to stop us."

"It could have been worse, much worse." Heather didn't like the picture her own words painted.

Gregg had another thought. "How are we going to transfer any Bibles now? They'll be watching us like hawks."

As if to confirm what he was saying, he glanced again into the rear view mirror. Nobody seemed to be following them. There were cars behind, but none seemed to be specifically attached to them.

At the Snow Road exit near Cleveland Gregg saw a sign which gave him an idea. He turned west toward the airport, all the time checking to see whether they were being followed. Nothing, or was there? He was still uncertain when he turned off the Airport Freeway toward the terminal.

"Take all my change out of my coat," he told Heather. "Then get in the back and lift the overnighter up here. It'll be heavy—I put all the Bibles in it."

She unfastened her seat belt, worked her way between the seats, and wrestled the small suitcase up front.

Gregg kept talking. "Find an empty locker. You may have to look around, but there ought to be one in there someplace. All we have to do tonight is give Nick the key. He or Pat can pick up the Bibles tomorrow."

Gregg stopped in front of the terminal. Heather tried to protest, but he would not hear it. "Go on. I'll pick you up right here."

Smothering her fear, Heather got out of the car, carrying the overnighter, and disappeared into the terminal. Gregg laughed at her efforts to hide how heavy the case was.

He took his time making the circuit, but when he came around Heather had not returned yet. Nothing to do but go around again, not so leisurely this time. She was waiting, empty-handed, when he came back.

"Got it?" he asked as she closed her door.

"Here it is, love," she said, holding the key out to him.

"You keep it," he suggested, trying to find an opening in the stream of traffic. "Now to get to Lakewood."

"Do you know these people we're going to see?"

"Yes, he's an engineer."

"Is he a minister, too?"

"No, Nick isn't a preacher, though he could be. Remember when I came down last summer? Part of that time I was with Nick. We may have talked about him."

"Is he the one who had the camp?"

"That's right. He arranged to take a bunch of kids to this public campground, but it actually was like a church camp. We had seventy-eight kids there, all high schoolers. Nick spoke five nights on the hundred and thirty-ninth Psalm.

"He said they don't give him too much trouble at his work. He knows his stuff so well they can't afford to, I suppose. He probably could get a better job, but because he's a believer they keep him where he is. That doesn't bother Nick, or Pat either."

Gregg tried to remember his directions, but nothing looked familiar. Older apartments bordered the slushy streets, the snow alongside the road pushed into dirty mounds.

"This doesn't seem right," he said to Heather. "I must have come too far." Gregg stopped at a filling station.

Heather got out and went to the ladies' room. When she stepped inside the station to return the key, Gregg was in conversation with the attendant. He had drawn his mark on the back of a magazine lying on the counter, and the attendant was asking about it.

"Does it give you any ideas?" Gregg asked.

"Looks like a boat, or part of a circle. Is that a sign of some kind?"

Gregg took the pencil and drew the other arc. "Now what does it look like?"

"It's a fish."

Gregg waited, but the attendant merely looked again at the drawing and back to Gregg. "Is it supposed to mean something?"

"Do you know Greek?"

"Does it have something to do with astrology?"

Heather tried to catch her husband's eye. She shook her head negatively, but Gregg ignored her. He looked out front to see whether there were any cars coming into the station.

"This is a sign the early Christians used," he explained to the man. "The first letter of each word in the sentence, 'Jesus Christ the Son of God,' makes the word 'fish' in Greek. So the Christians used the fish as their sign during the days when they had to meet in secret. Do you get it now?"

Suddenly the man was interested. "So that means you're a Christian?"

Gregg looked at Heather again. He could tell she was afraid. "Yes, we are. My wife and I are both followers of Jesus."

The man looked at Gregg. "You really believe that stuff, don't you?"

His question took Gregg aback. "Yes, we really do."

"I used to go to church myself," the attendant said. "I used to go with my grandma, years ago."

A car drove up out front, and Gregg realized their conversation was finished. "May we give you something?" he asked quickly. Then, to Heather, "Let's give our friend a present."

Again, that nearly imperceptible negative from Heather. Gregg spoke again. "We want to leave you a gift."

Heather took a deep breath, reached into her purse, and handed Gregg one of the little black books. Quickly Gregg put the Bible into the front pocket of the attendant's jacket. He patted the man's jacket as he turned to leave. "Read it, my friend. It can change your life."

Moments later they were back on the main street. "Do you know what?" Gregg nearly shouted. "I got so wrapped up in giving him that Bible I forgot to ask for directions."

"Love, I don't feel so well."

"Hey"—Gregg reached over to her—"my girl's getting hungry. We're going to have to take care of my girl."

The next signal light turned red, and as Gregg came to a stop he recognized the cross street. "I know where we are now," he told Heather. "Let's make a quick stop at the Mattinglys', and then we'll go have us a good lunch and be on our way."

"And start home?" she said, hopefully.

Gregg hesitated to commit himself. "We'll head that direction. Let's not make any final decision till we see how we feel tonight after we've seen Brother Ellis."

"Gregg, I'm scared. I didn't like it back there at that filling station, I don't like it when police cars stop us, I don't like being followed. I feel so trapped. I don't know if I dare stay here another night."

He laid his hand on hers. "Hon, one more night. That's all I ask. Then we go home."

Heather's eyes brimmed, and a tear ran down her cheek. "I'm so scared, Gregg. I'm not sure I can take it another hour."

"I know, hon." He was reading street markers as they drove along. "Let's go see Nick and Pat, and then we'll start home."

"I feel so ashamed"—Heather sniffled as she talked—"to feel this way. I've been here only a week and I can hardly manage. How do these people stand it?"

Gregg turned down a side street, went a couple of blocks, and slipped in back of a twelve-story high rise.

He buzzed the wall button for Apartment 207. No answer. Blocked by the security door, he was unsure what to do.

"How can we get inside?" Heather wanted to know.

"Wait a couple of minutes," he suggested, "until someone comes out."

Heather felt as if she were on display, though there was no one around. "Gregg," she pleaded, "can't we leave?"

"I've got an idea," he said, looking again at the board listing the names and numbers of the people living in the apartment. "Watch this," he said to his wife.

He pushed a button at random and waited. No answer. He selected another one. Again, no answer. When he pushed 1014, a woman's voice came over the intercom.

"Yes?"

"Parcel for Schreiber," Gregg said reading the name from the board beside the call button.

There was a moment's silence, then the sound of the electric switch unlocking the front door. The speaker rasped, "Come in."

He grabbed Heather's hand and led her through. She didn't like it at all. "Gregg, that was wrong." He laughed, which made her even more upset. He was still chuckling to himself when they stepped off the elevator at the second floor. No one answered their knock, so Gregg wrote a note and tried to slip it underneath the door.

He finally succeeded in working the paper through the narrow space, but there was no way he could ever get the locker key through. They would have to come back.

"Let's go see what the lake is like," Gregg suggested as they rode down in the elevator.

At the apartment the drive to the lake had sounded like a good idea, but staring at the water only made Heather more homesick.

"It looks cold, doesn't it?" Gregg observed.

"Not very friendly, either," she said, watching the sleek patrol yacht slowly zig-zag in regular rhythm. Built on the style of a luxury cabin cruiser, its gray paint and the deck gun showed its true identity.

The wind coming off the lake dropped the temperature two or three degrees, so Heather was glad when they started the car and headed back toward Nick and Pat's.

"Some town, isn't it?" Gregg commented to his companion as they turned back toward the city. The car behind him had turned, too.

"This must be an older section."

The other car was still behind them. Probably nothing to worry about. It looked like an ordinary sedan. Then Gregg saw that the driver was holding a hand microphone. Must be a CB operator. Did they even have CB's down here any more? Gregg wasn't sure. He was sure of one thing. Don't let on to Heather.

"Traffic's not too bad, is it?" he said, hoping his voice didn't betray his uneasiness.

Then he saw the roadblock.

Two police cars idled on the right side of the street, their pursuit lights flashing red, the drivers in both cars alert and ready for instant chase. Just as the Volvo approached, a third car pulled across the road, completely blocking the street. Uniformed men were everywhere, with one officer standing by the first car, motioning for Gregg to stop.

Heather screamed. The moment the car stopped, they were surrounded and Gregg's door was jerked open.

"Get out."

Heather's door, too, was open and she was ordered out.

Gregg tried to find his tongue. "What's wrong? What's this all about?"

Gregg managed to keep his footing as the officer pulled him out of the car and shoved him against the fender. As directed, he put his hands on the hood and spread his legs while the officer frisked him for weapons.

"Get your hands off her. Get your filthy hands off her." Even as Gregg tried to come to Heather's aid, strong hands restrained him and held him prisoner.

"Get in that car," the officer commanded. Gregg knew it was useless to resist.

He did manage to ask, "Do we take our coats?"

The officer nodded and Gregg turned toward the car, but was instantly stopped. One hand on his pistol, the officer pointed with the other toward the police car. "Let's go. We'll get the coats. Move."

Traffic had come to a halt and people were staring. Gregg's face burned, more with indignation than embarrassment. He started to say something to his wife but thought better of it, intimidated by the burly figure crowding him toward the patrol car.

The officer opened the door, and Gregg slid into the back seat. Satisfied that neither of the prisoners' coats carried weapons, the deputy threw them in on top of Gregg and slammed the door. Heather got in from the other side. An officer on the passenger side in the front did not even turn around.

Gregg saw to his horror that there were no handles either on his or Heather's door, nor were there any turn cranks for their windows. Between themselves and the uniformed figure in the front seat rose a heavy barrier of steel mesh.

Gregg felt suddenly hot, cramped. He couldn't breathe. Glancing at his wife, he saw that she was experiencing the same sensation.

The car had a metallic, oily smell. Up front the radio spoke in quick, short phrases. Subconsciously Gregg deciphered the terse messages, but his mind was elsewhere. He kept clenching and unclenching his fist, then caught himself and stopped.

He reached across and tried to take Heather's hand, but she pulled it away. Her eyes were shut tight, and she was shaking her head from side to side.

Across the street a crowd of bystanders had gathered, held back by the shouting policeman directing traffic. The car blocking the road had been moved to one side and traffic had started to flow again, but other drivers slowed to gawk. People stared out the windows of an apartment building down the block.

Gregg leaned forward to speak to the officer up front. "Did we do something wrong? Were we going too fast?" he asked through the grating.

Gregg meant for his voice to sound confident, but the words came out more like a croak. The officer did not even acknowledge the questions.

Gregg started to make another attempt, then sank back into the seat. A sergeant opened the driver's door and got into the car. "Nothing in their car," he said to his partner.

"Should I drive it?"

"No, let Ferguson follow us. You radio headquarters and tell them we're on our way."

Gregg leaned forward again. "Could someone tell us what's wrong? What did we do? We can explain."

His voice trailed off. Neither officer paid him any attention. Gregg turned around and looked out the back window. He felt sick as he watched another policeman get into the Volvo and start the motor. Then they started to move.

Gregg could not bear to look at Heather. He kept staring out his side window, looking at the buildings, the passing cars, street signs. Heather touched his arm and he jumped, hoping the policemen up front had not seen the movement.

Then Gregg saw the tiny object in Heather's hand—the locker key from the airport. What could they do with it? Could they get rid of it somehow?

He gingerly inched his hand across the seat toward her, then pulled his hand back and motioned for her to put the key down inside her boot. Somehow he felt better. At least he had done something. A small enough act, but it was something.

They were being taken toward the city. Gregg turned

around to look behind again; the Volvo was still following them. The sky was lighter behind them than it was ahead. Before long it would be dark.

The road opened up to give them a clear view of Cleveland. At any other time Gregg might have thought the scene spectacular, but not now. Moments later they were lost in the dark downtown canyons.

Gregg could tell they were close to their destination even before they reached it. The officer in the passenger seat spoke into the hand microphone, giving their location and telling the dispatcher to ready the door. The driver made one complete circuit of a block enclosing an enormous mass marked Department of Security, then turned in toward a door which parted on signal.

The prisoners found themselves in a small, open courtyard. A row of stunted trees huddled against the far wall, out of place amidst the marble and concrete. Were it not for the bright lights, the area would have been in shadow.

Gregg was so intent on their surroundings he did not feel the car brake to a stop. His Volvo pulled up beside them.

"Get out," came the command as their car doors opened. "Follow me."

What else could they do? Their escort led them past a guard, through double doors into a reception area.

"Looks like a hospital," Gregg whispered to his wife, relieved. This wouldn't be so bad. Their footsteps were hushed on the carpeted floor. Heather noticed several paintings hanging around the room.

"This way."

They entered a smaller room, also carpeted, with drapes which matched the rug. The soft glow from a table lamp blended pleasantly with the pastel walls and the last of the daylight coming through the window. Two guards stood at rigid attention beside the door, but the man behind the desk seemed relaxed enough. His uniform was green.

"Please be seated," he said, offering them chairs.

For several moments he said nothing, his eyes first on Gregg, then on Heather. In the silence Gregg could hear Heather's quick breathing.

Finally the man behind the desk spoke. Not until that moment had Gregg realized that there, on the desk in front of the officer, was a Bible, a little Bible like those in Heather's purse.

"It seems we have a problem," the officer began, noting with satisfaction that Gregg was staring at the Bible. "We have here two guests in our country, two visitors to the Democratic Republic of America, two friends here through the courtesy of our government, and they are openly and intentionally disobeying our laws."

Gregg kept silent, his eyes intent on the little black volume on the desk.

The officer kept looking at him. "Who are you and what are you doing in the D.R.A?"

"I am Gregg Richards," he began slowly. "This is my wife, Heather."

"I'm Captain Stocker. Please continue."

"We've been married four months. We came down for the holidays."

"I see. On vacation, is that it?"

"Yes, sir."

"Go on."

"We came to visit my folks."

Stocker's eyebrows lifted at that. "You have family here?"

Gregg felt as if he were slipping down the sides of a steep pit. Could he keep from falling? "They'd never met Heather and I wanted them to meet, I mean, her to meet them."

The man behind the desk pursed his lips. "I see. And you've spent the holidays with them?"

"Yes. I mean, not all the time. We visited them, yes."

"And you've been sightseeing the remainder of the time?"

"Yes, sir."

Deliberately, Captain Stocker pushed his chair away from the desk and stood up. He picked up the little book and turned it over in his hands, looking at it, opening the pages, riffling them with his thumb.

Without warning he threw the book directly at Gregg, hitting him full in the chest, and shouted, "Then what is this?"

Gregg flinched as if he'd been lashed with a whip. Stocker

came around and stood over Gregg. He stared down at him and repeated his question, "Tell me, what is this? What is the meaning of this?"

"If we did something wrong, we didn't mean any trouble."

Gregg's explanation infuriated the man. The captain's face became livid. "*If* you did something wrong. So you didn't mean trouble. Young man, you cannot come to our country and start passing out Bibles as if they were door prizes. Do you understand?"

Surely everyone in the reception area and the hallways could hear. Stocker put his face close to Gregg's. "How many more of these things do you have?"

Gregg struggled for control. "Heather has a few in her purse. That's all."

"How many?"

Stocker turned to Heather, who opened her purse and took out the last of the little books, which Stocker threw on his desk. He turned and spoke to one of the guards. "My coat please. I want to have a look at their car."

Turning back to Gregg, he said, "You two come with me."

The two forlorn captives fell in between two guards who escorted them back outside. It was much colder than before; darker, too.

Moving with practiced efficiency, a team of examiners descended on the station wagon. Gregg could only watch, grimly fascinated. He moved closer to Heather, careful to notice whether the guards might object, but no one paid him any attention. All eyes were on the car. Armed figures perched at regular stations on the wall surrounding the courtyard.

In seconds the glove box was emptied, the door pockets searched, and the front seat cushions removed. One man was down on his knees, feeling underneath the seats to see if there was anything underneath the carpeting. Another examiner opened the engine hood.

Gregg watched the man up front, and tensed when the inspector's eyes narrowed as he bent for a closer look at the wiring. The man straightened up and looked directly at Gregg, then moved to the front seat. The two men began probing under the dash. Gregg could hear their exclamation when they found the transceiver equipment.

Heather turned and buried her face in Gregg's coat, sobbing. He said nothing as he stroked her hair. Even through his heavy coat he could feel her trembling body, then realized he was shaking, too. He couldn't bring himself to look at her, but kept watching the methodical violation of his car.

Captain Stocker stood a little apart, watching Gregg as much as the two men working on the car. They had the back open now. Quickly the center compartment was emptied, then the right side storage area. The suitcase, the clothes on hangers, and Gregg's extra oil were scattered out onto the concrete.

Now the man was unscrewing the hold-downs for the spare tire cover. With the cover laid to one side, he reached into the cavity with a flashlight, groping, peering down into every crevice.

His hand dove inside and came back triumphant: a Bible. It must have dropped between the fender well and the quarter panel back at the filling station in Coryville.

Coryville. That was years ago, Gregg thought.

Captain Stocker snorted, "So you came down to visit family, did you? I suggest you come back to my office and tell me what you really came down here for."

Stocker snapped his fingers to the two guards, who fell in with the prisoners and brought them back inside again.

Now Stocker became all business. "Richards, let me hear your story from the beginning. When did you come? Where did you go? Whom did you see? What did you do?"

This time he did not offer them a seat. Gregg forced himself to act calm, to stand still and look the Captain in the eye.

"We came, as I told you, a week ago Friday. We stayed outside Buffalo. I should have said, we crossed at the Peace Bridge. Then we stayed outside Buffalo. Saturday we stayed in Ohio, and Sunday . . . let's see, that was the

twenty-third. We stayed at this real nice place Christmas
Eve, then with my folks on Chris—, I mean, on the
twenty-fifth. Then we crossed over into West Virginia. We
went to Hawk's Nest and the capitol. Then we drove to
Kentucky and came back to Ohio and now we're on our
way home, back to Toronto."

Captain Stocker glared at Gregg in disgust. "Do you
actually think for one minute that I have the slightest
interest in a recital like that? What I want to know is,
Where did you go? Whom did you see? What did you do?
Perhaps if you try again, you can remember."

Gregg found himself wishing for a drink of water. The
captain sipped a cup of coffee and waited.

"We saw lots of things. My wife's an artist, and she likes
to draw. You could see her drawings, sir, out in the car.
We stopped at this old cabin, this log cabin, and she made a
sketch of that, and then in West Virginia she . . . "

"Enough." Stocker cut him short. "I don't want to hear
it." He studied Gregg, then his gaze went to Heather, then
back to Gregg.

"Richards," he said, scorn heavy in his voice, "you seem
to be a bright boy. You certainly don't want to spend the
rest of the night standing there trying to make up answers
to my questions. My questions aren't all that difficult, are
they?"

He waited, allowing his words to sink in.

"Perhaps you have forgotten them already. I know you
have probably driven a long way today. You must be tired,
and thinking of bed and a good night's rest. Perhaps a
shower; a hot, relaxing shower. So that I might refresh your
memory, may I repeat my questions one at a time. Where
did you go? Whom did you see? What did you do?"

"Sir," Gregg answered him, "I am trying to tell you. We
crossed at the Peace Bridge and stayed the first night in a
motel outside Buffalo. Saturday we drove across and came
into Ohio and . . . "

Stocker waved for Gregg to stop. Placing both palms flat
on the desk, he leaned across and threw the words at Gregg.
"You're a fool." Then he demanded, "Give me your papers."

The captain accepted the two passports and visas and

thumbed through the papers, comparing the photographs with the two tired faces in front of him.

Stocker laid everything down, then picked up Gregg's passport and flourished it in front of him. "You know this is no good, don't you?"

"Sir," Gregg began, "that is still a valid passport."

"So you say. This is out of date, young man. You're behind the times."

"Sir," Gregg insisted, "I've been here before with this passport. I've never had any trouble before."

Stocker snorted. "I'll say you haven't. You've never been in trouble because you've never been caught. But you're in trouble now."

He turned in his chair to the credenza beside his desk, slid a panel aside, and exposed what appeared to be a television screen and typewriter. Looking at Gregg's passport, Stocker keyed a series of letters and numbers and waited for the image to form.

"So I see. So I see. Looks as if I've landed a big fish, a very big fish."

Gregg saw Heather just in time and reached her as she swayed and collapsed. She would have slumped to the floor had he not caught her. Gregg eased her into one of the chairs and loosened her coat, supporting her so she wouldn't fall forward.

Captain Stocker spoke to one of the guards, and within moments a woman attendant appeared with water and smelling salts. Heather came around slowly, color reappearing in her cheeks.

"Why don't you take her down the hall," Stocker said to the woman. Heather registered alarm, but before she could resist she was helped from the room.

Why was Heather limping? Gregg watched his wife until she was gone. Stocker brought him back to the matter at hand.

"Richards, why don't you make yourself at home. You'll be here a while. According to that sheet, I'm supposed to notify Washington about you."

When his secretary finally tracked him down, Bert Wilson was celebrating New Year's two days early. Wilson's irritation at being summoned from the party melted when he heard what Captain Joseph Stocker told him over the telephone.

"Got him right there in Cleveland, you say . . . ? Yeah . . . We had him in West Virginia and then lost him . . . Bibles? In a compartment? . . . I'm coming up there, Stocker . . . No, don't apologize. I'll have a man fly me down tonight. That's no problem. I want to see this one myself, hear? Hold on to him, Stocker. Got that?"

Before dawn, Sunday, December 30

Without his watch, Gregg had no way to keep track of the hours. They had taken everything: belt, shoelaces, billfold, comb, keys, pen, wristwatch, and the little penknife he always carried. Pacing back and forth in his cramped cell, he had to concentrate to keep from stepping out of his shoes.

Evidently he was in a special cell. He had room enough—three paces forward, one sideways, three back—but in this block there were only his and the empty cell next to him. The two compartments faced a fairly large anteroom, where a battered desk dominated the open area and a heavy bench sat against one wall. The only other person within Gregg's range of vision was a guard at the desk, working on a stack of papers.

Gregg was determined to figure out a way to mark the passage of time. He tried taking his pulse, but lost track when he began walking back and forth. Trying again, he counted under his breath, maintaining the same rhythm as his heartbeat, and stepped his three forward and one to the side and three back. Again.

Seven seconds? Six? Maybe five? Allowing five seconds to make one circuit of the cell, that meant twelve circuits would count for one minute, and in ten minutes he could walk 120 laps.

The guard worked with his back to Gregg, but looked
over his shoulder and checked the prisoner from time to
time. Gregg stopped every time he thought the guard might
look around.

He could use the Lord's Prayer. Didn't it take three
minutes to say it through one time? No. Couldn't be.
Maybe three times through added up to one minute. Better
forget that.

Sounds were so difficult to identify. Far away he could
hear muffled voices, but try as he might he could not decide
whether they were conversation or a radio or what. Once he
heard what sounded like a scream, but he put that thought
out of his mind immediately.

Nothing to do but keep pacing and thinking—and praying.

Hearing footsteps, Gregg pressed his face against the bars
of his cell and strained to get a glimpse of whoever was
coming into the outer room. Without ceremony a guard
walked up to the desk and deposited a pair of boots and
knit socks, and went back the direction he came. The boots
and socks were Heather's.

Gregg gripped the bars, wanting to scream. Desperately
he pulled at the unyielding metal as if, Samson-like, he
could bend the steel.

"Dear God," he sobbed under his breath, "don't let them
do anything to Heather. Please." He crouched against the
back wall and beat his fists against the concrete.

"Dear God, dear God; don't let them do anything to
Heather. Please, God. It's my fault we're here. Don't let
them do anything to her, God, please."

The sound of regular tapping gradually penetrated his
consciousness and he turned to see the guard standing
outside his cell, striking a ball-point pen lightly against the
bars.

"Mister Richards," the guard told him, "I wouldn't let
them see me doing that, if I were you. You'd better stand
up or sit on your bunk." The guard pointed to a closed
circuit camera in the ceiling which Gregg hadn't noticed
before.

Wearily he got to his feet and resumed pacing, only to
stop when he remembered the camera. When he sat on the

bunk, he could see Heather's boots and socks, and that made it worse. Gregg looked at the slimy floor, then stood up and began pacing again, praying silently.

It had to be an hour, perhaps closer to two when he heard footsteps out in the hallway again. They belonged to the same guard, only this time he carried a suitcase. Gregg gasped as he recognized their overnighter.

The guard lifted it to the desk top, next to the boots, and walked away. Gregg stared in numb disbelief. So they had found the key, they had been to the airport. What else had they done? What else?

The solitary guard in the outer room got up and left, leaving Gregg entirely alone. Another hour passed, maybe longer. If there were only some way to measure time. Gregg determined not to succumb to his feeling of helplessness.

Footsteps again. This time it was Captain Stocker. Stocker glanced at the objects on the desk as he walked by, then approached Gregg's cell and stood, waiting.

"Well?" Stocker asked.

Gregg looked past him at the things on the desk.

Stocker tried again. "Has your memory improved, Richards?"

Gregg could not trust himself to answer.

"You know what I want," the Captain repeated. "Where did you go? Whom did you see? What did you do with those Bibles?"

Still Gregg did not answer. Stocker stood there a few moments, then left. The guard returned, this time carrying a sandwich and something to drink. In spite of himself, Gregg felt his mouth begin to water. He was only fifteen feet from where the man was eating. The sandwich was roast beef, on whole wheat bread, with mayonnaise. And a Coke. A tall, cold Coca-Cola.

Gregg took his three steps forward, one to the side, three back, to the side again, three forward. He had long ceased caring whether the guard saw him or what the closed circuit camera showed.

Throughout the night Gregg kept praying one prayer over and over: that God would let nothing happen to Heather.

During intervals in his prayer, Gregg quoted Scripture to himself, every verse he could remember.

Several hours later Stocker appeared again, this time accompanied by a waddling hulk of a man. The grotesque newcomer trailed smoke from a cigar as thick as one of his fat fingers.

Stocker made the introductions. "Mr. Wilson, take a look at Gregg Richards."

Wilson studied Gregg like an auctioneer sizing up an animal for the block. Grunting, Wilson directed Stocker to have the guard bring over the bench. The two men moved the heavy piece of furniture, and Wilson settled his bulk opposite the prisoner.

"Looks as if you've had a bad night, Richards," Wilson began. "Suppose you start at the beginning and tell us about yourself."

Gregg said nothing.

"As I said"—Wilson ground on in his raspy voice—"you've had a rough night. But it's going to get rougher if you don't cooperate."

Mentally Gregg kept repeating the Twenty-third Psalm to himself over and over. Waiting, Wilson glowered at him. Gregg shut his eyes so he could not see the huge head and the brutish stare. Wilson summoned him back to reality.

"In case you don't know, Richards," Wilson told him, "I'm getting tired of waiting. Very tired of waiting."

His throat dry, Gregg asked, "What do you want?"

"That's better. Start at the beginning and tell us who you are and what you're doing in the D.R.A."

Gregg's voice made a ringing sound in his ears as he tried to put the words together. "My name is Gregg Richards. We live in Mississauga, Ontario. My wife's name is Heather. We came to visit my parents. They had never met her. We left Canada Friday a week ago. We stayed in a motel west of Buffalo, off the Thruway. Saturday we drove across Pennsylvania. We stayed five nights in Ohio, then crossed into West Virginia. We . . ."

Wilson stopped him. "Shut up with that nonsense. Look, we know all about you. We could put your story together for the national news. Stocker here says you're having trouble remembering. Maybe we ought to help you."

Gregg swallowed. "What do you need to know?" If he could only bargain for time, for an opening, some way to get the two of them out of this.

"I want to know who you gave those Bibles to. I want to know how you got their names and addresses. I want to know who else is working with you." He leaned back and blew a cloud of smoke at the ceiling.

"The last part is easy," Gregg began. "We don't work with anyone. We came here by ourselves."

For a big man, Wilson moved surprisingly fast. Before Gregg could dodge, Wilson stood up and spat full in his face. "You make me puke. Who do you think you're trying to fool? There's a pack of you scum who sneak in here and peddle your black market Bibles to our people. Don't try to fool me."

"Sir," Gregg told him, "I'm telling you God's truth. I'm not with anyone else. Heather and I came on our own."

Wilson howled. "God's truth. Ha! You can stick that with your black market Bibles."

Gregg tried again. "Sir, it's the truth. I had Bibles, yes, but I gave them away. I didn't sell a single Bible. I gave every one of them away."

Wilson exploded again. "That's rich. You're stupid for bringing in Bibles, even more stupid for not selling them."

He slapped Stocker on the back, and the two of them enjoyed the joke. Shifting his weight to a more comfortable position, Wilson resumed his task. "Point number one: you're stupid. Point number two: you're in trouble. Point number three: you've got your girl friend in a lot of trouble. Don't you care about her, Richards?"

Wilson sucked on his cigar and let Gregg think about that one. His eyes kept boring into Gregg, studying his reactions. Wilson leaned forward and exhaled a lungful of smoke, making the prisoner turn his face away.

"Now let's see if you can remember where you went and who you saw. We put together your route, so we already have a good idea, but you can make it easier for yourself if you help us nail this down tight."

Gregg said nothing.

Wilson persisted. "Listen, I came a long way to get this chance with you. I'm not leaving until I get what I came for."

Gregg remained silent.

Wilson looked at Stocker, then turned to the desk behind him and picked up one of Heather's boots. He held it at arm's length and dropped it, the sound reverberating dully down the long hallway. After the echo had faded, Wilson picked up the other boot and dropped it, then stared at Gregg.

Gregg clenched the bars. He was shaking uncontrollably.

Abruptly Wilson moved to leave and beckoned for Stocker to follow. Gregg strained to hear what they were saying as they left the room, but all he could make out were the words, "the girl."

When they came back a long time afterward, Gregg was still clutching the cell bars, staring, his lips moving. This time Wilson didn't sit down. Stocker pointed a recording device at Gregg as Wilson came to the point at once.

"Look, Richards, I hate to tell you, but your girl friend spilled her guts. She sang such a nice song, we decided to let her go home. Only one problem. If you want to take what's left of her back across that border, you're going to have to make it a duet.

"What we've got on this tape is her account of where you went and what you did. She was a little rusty in spots —maybe we helped her too much—so we need you to fill in the blanks. You just speak right here into this microphone. If everything matches, the two of you can go back where you came from."

Gregg missed part of the speech. Retching, he turned his back and was sick. Wilson looked at Stocker and sat down to wait. Ten minutes later, Gregg pulled himself together and started talking.

Sunday, December 30

Gregg combed his hair into place, grateful for the warm water, fresh towels, and razor. He tried not to think of last night.

The guard snapped his fingers, signaling the prisoner to get a move on. Gregg took another look in the mirror and stepped out into the hallway.

Heather was sitting by the door, silhouetted in the sunlight. Adorable, lovely Heather. He crushed her to himself, then took a step back and looked at her again, unbelieving.

It couldn't be . . . The guards were rushing them through the doorway and outside into the courtyard. Was it only last night they were brought into this place?

Wilson was standing by the Volvo with the tailgate open, and their overnighter broken apart, and the Bibles scattered about the car's cargo area. Wilson told a guard who was carrying a five-liter can of gasoline, "Pour it on. Use it all."

Gregg watched helplessly, powerless to move. Heather stood next to him. The guard moved toward the car, but as he lifted the can Wilson stopped him. Pointing a stubby forefinger, Wilson said, "I've changed my mind. We won't burn the car, only the Bibles."

Wilson leaned his bulk inside the car and scraped the Bibles out onto the ground and kicked them into a pile a short distance away. Then, as Wilson directed, the guard emptied the gasoline onto the heap.

Suddenly inspired, Wilson brought out a sheaf of papers from his coat pocket and loftily dropped them one by one onto the gasoline-soaked pyre. Gregg lunged forward, but a guard caught him.

"Our papers," Gregg shouted.

Wilson motioned to the guard, and instantly the mound whooshed into flame. Gregg and Heather stared numbly. Wilson let the fire burn until most of the Bibles were consumed, then turned to the girl and her dazed husband.

"You're down here with no papers now. One false move and the two of you will never see daylight again. I'm letting you go, but you better see how straight you can make for the Peace Bridge. Once you get over there, I better never see you down here with Bibles again. Never."

The two dispirited figures nodded silently. Neither said a word until they were several blocks away from the Security Building.

"You look a sight, love," Heather said gently.

"What did they do to you?" he asked, searching her face. His question surprised her. "Nothing."

"Did they hurt you?"

"Me? No, love. Did they you?"

"What . . . what did you tell them?"

Gregg's question cut Heather like a jagged knife. She looked at him curiously. "I didn't tell them anything, love."

"We don't have to hold back from each other."

Stung, she recoiled in dismay. "Hold back what? What do you mean, Gregg?"

"Wilson said you told him everything."

"Wilson?" Heather didn't understand. "Gregg, I was terrified, but I didn't tell them a thing. God help me, I didn't tell them a thing."

She twisted around until her face was almost in front of his. "I didn't, love. I didn't tell them anything."

From deep in his soul Gregg yielded a sob of agony. Suddenly Heather understood, her eyes wide, her mouth gaping.

"Gregg, they didn't make you . . ."

She couldn't bring herself to finish such an awful thought. But her eyes, fixed on Gregg's face, told her enough.

Heedless of the oncoming traffic, Gregg bent his head to the wheel, unwilling to see or be seen. Heather couldn't look at him now, couldn't bear to see her husband's anguish, so naked and exposed. Zombie-like, Gregg drove. Except for the slight motion of his hands guiding the wheel, he resembled a corpse.

"I hate myself," he said finally, his voice nearly inaudible. Starting to sob again, he went on, "I betrayed God's people."

Cleveland slipped astern. Then Willoughby, Painesville, Geneva. Mechanically Gregg followed I-90 along the road they had come, past the same desolate farms, the same snow-covered fields. This time Heather showed no interest in the scenery.

Desperately she sought for words to comfort her husband. She looked at the car, his car, the car he had been so proud to buy, the one he had been so pleased to take her places in. Now its dash was ripped apart where the short-wave had been torn out, its upholstery slashed to ribbons, the cargo area and the back seat in shreds. Even their one remaining suitcase was ruined.

Gregg was ripped apart, too, by whatever had happened last night. They were adrift on the open sea, without papers, without permission, with no port should they or the car need assistance.

The highway signs marked their silent passage. At the Pennsylvania border Gregg slowed, but the guards waved them on through. Evidently they were expected.

Still Gregg drove in silence, staring. Nothing she could say seemed to penetrate his shame.

They crested a rise overlooking the lake. Across the median a snow plow trailed its veil of white. Straight and satiny, I-90 stretched away to infinity.

Heather tried again. She had to. "Love"—she put her arm around him, grasped his shoulder tightly—"don't you see what they did? It wasn't just the names. They wanted to destroy you; they wanted to destroy us."

He drove on, listening but not answering.

"We're the enemy. They hate us, Gregg, because we're believers. That's why they did it. But it didn't work. They can't destroy my husband. He's too strong."

His reply was a groan. For a moment Heather feared to say anything more, but she had to keep trying.

"They can't destroy us, love. They can't. We still have the Lord. Don't you see, Gregg?"

Heather could see tears on his cheeks. She kept talking. "We still have the Lord, love. We still do."

He groped for her hand and held it as a drowning man would grab a lifeline.

"Yes," he repeated numbly, "we still have the Lord."

She brushed his cheek with kisses and stroked away his tears with her free hand. She was crying, too. "And we still have each other."

"Yes." Gregg's eyes finally met hers. "We have each other, we have the Lord, we have freedom."

For several minutes neither one said any more. Then Gregg broke the silence.

"If only I'd stood firm. I had my chance. Oh, if only I'd stood firm."

"Gregg," Heather cut him short, "think of them, too. Think of the people here. Not the ones we've been with—think of the others, so many of them. What if they'd stood firm when they had their chance?"

Gregg looked over at her again.

"You're right," he said slowly. "I guess that's always the problem, isn't it?"

The guard boats swam like angry beetles across the lake's smooth surface.

"Love," she offered, "let's go home."

"Right," he responded, his voice stronger now. He brought his speed up to the limit. "Let's go home."